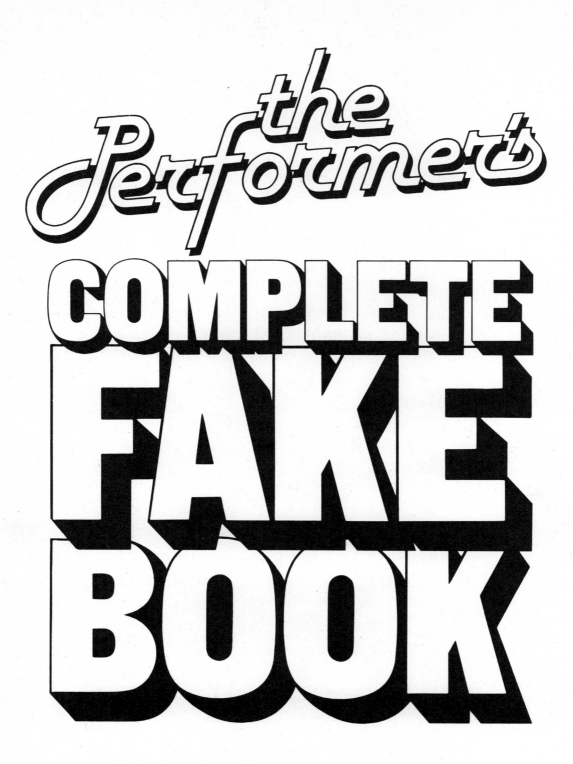

the Performer's COMPLETE FAKE BOOK

ATLANTIC PRODUCTION COMPANY

Exclusively distributed by

 HAL LEONARD
PUBLISHING
CORPORATION

Home Office: **National Sales Office:**
960 East Mark Street   8112 West Bluemound Road
Winona MN 55987   Milwaukee WI 53213

THE PERFORMER'S COMPLETE FAKE BOOK

CONTENTS

Alphabetical Listing

iv

Composer/Lyricist Index

In the following index, many of the prominent composers and lyricists whose music appears in this book are listed alphabetically with their compositions and the page number on which each song can be found.

Music Categories

The following index is a list of the many songs in this book which can be classified in categories of Music Styles & Tempos, hits of specific Recording Artists, Broadway Show Music and Motion Picture Music. Use this listing as a reference in preparing medleys or in finding favorite categories of music.

MUSIC STYLES & TEMPOS

RECORDING ARTISTS

BROADWAY SHOW MUSIC

AC-CENT-TCHU-ATE THE POSITIVE

(From the Motion Picture "Here Come The Waves")

Lyric by JOHNNY MERCER
Music by HAROLD ARLEN

ANGRY

Words by DUDLEY MECUM
Music by JULES CASSARD, HENRY BRUNIES
& MERRITT BRUNIES

ADELAIDE
(From "Guys And Dolls")

By FRANK LOESSER

AFTER THE BALL / MILLION MILES

Words and Music by
McCARTNEY

AIN'T THERE ANYONE HERE FOR LOVE?
(From the Motion Picture "Gentlemen Prefer Blondes")

Words by HAROLD ADAMSON
Music by HOAGY CARMICHAEL

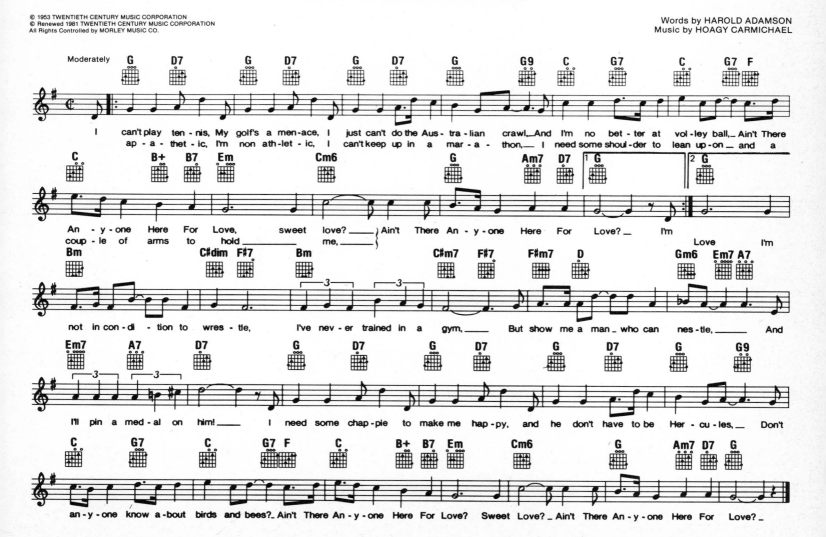

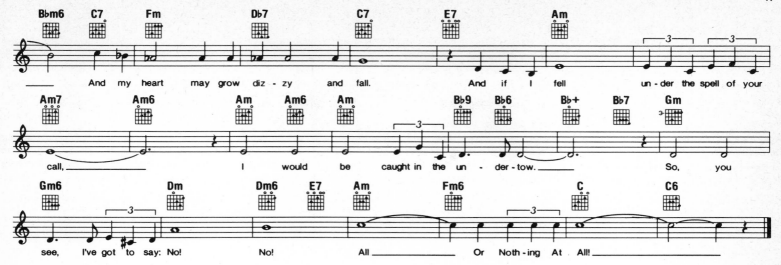

And my heart may grow diz-zy and fall. And if I fell un-der the spell of your

call, _____ I would be caught in the un-der-tow._____ So, you

see, I've got to say: No! No! All _____ Or Noth-ing At All! _____

ANY WHICH WAY YOU CAN

Words and Music by MILTON L. BROWN,
STEPHEN H. DORFF & SNUFF GARRETT

It's hard for a back street af-fair to be eas-y, for each hour of hap-pi-ness there's two hours of pain._ But we

meet in th shad-ows___ be-cause all _ that mat-ters is spend-ing the night _____ with each oth-er a-gain._ You'll

leave with a prom-ise___ that you'll call me to-mor-row,___ but I nev-er know _____ when the next time will be._ And

each time you leave_ me my heart_ keeps re-peat-ing,___ was last night the last_ night ____ for you and for _ me? ___

An-y Which Way You_ Can, Just love me An-y Which Way You_ Can. My loves. not the chok-in' kind, ___

You've got your life and I've_ got _mine. I know you can nev-er be free, And ba-by I un-der _ stand.

But when you're_ ly-ing next to me, _____ just love me An-y Which Way You_ Can. Now you're

2. Now you're on your way home
leavin' me all alone,
feeling almost as empty as this
big double bed.

And it's hard to be strong
when I know I belong
in your arms, but I'm lying
here lonely instead.

AT THE HOP

Words and Music by A. SINGER
J. MEDORA & D. WHITE

ANOTHER SLEEPLESS NIGHT

Words and Music by RORY BOURKE & CHARLIE BLACK

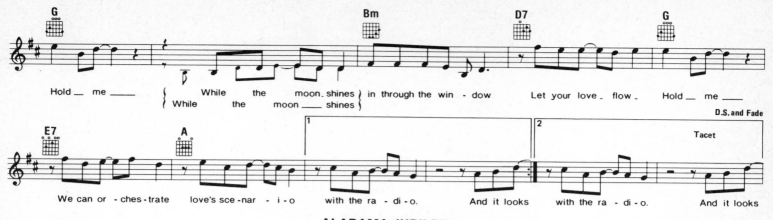

Hold __ me _____ { While the moon shines } in through the win - dow Let your love flow. Hold me ____
{ While the moon shines }

D.S. and Fade

We can or - ches - trate love's sce - nar - i - o with the ra - di - o. And it looks with the ra - di - o. And it looks

ALABAMA JUBILEE

Words by JACK YELLEN
Music by GEORGE L. COBB

You ought to see Mis - ter Jones__ when he rat - tles the bones,__ Old Colo - nel Brown__ fool - in' 'round like a clown,__

__ Miss Vir - gin - ia who is past eight - y three,__ Shout - in' "I'm full __ o' pep! Watch yo' step, watch __

(Spoken)

__ yo' step!" One leg - ged Joe danced a - roun' on his toe, __ Threw a - way his crutch and hol - lered, "Let 'er go!" __

Oh, hon - ey, Hail! Hail! the gang's all here for an Al - a - ba - ma Jub - i - lee.

ACROSS THE FIELD

Words and Music by
W.A. DOUGHERTY, JR.

Fight that team A-cross The Field, Show them O - hi - o's here. ____ Set the earth re - ver - ber -

a - ting with a might - y cheer Rah! Rah! Rah! Hit them hard and see how they fall; Nev - er let that

team get the ball, Hail! Hail! the gang's all here, So let's beat { that Ill - i - ni now. (Yell) O - O -
{ In - di - a - na now.

hi - o! O - O - hi - o! Wa - hoo! Wa - hoo! for O - hi - o!

D.C. al Fine

ALONE TOO LONG
(From the Broadway Musical "By The Beautiful Sea")

Words by DOROTHY FIELDS
Music by ARTHUR SCHWARTZ

ALRIGHT, OKAY, YOU WIN

Words and Music by
SID WYCHE & MAYME WATTS

ANNIE
(From the Musical Production "Annie")

Words by MARTIN CHARNIN
Music by CHARLES STROUSE

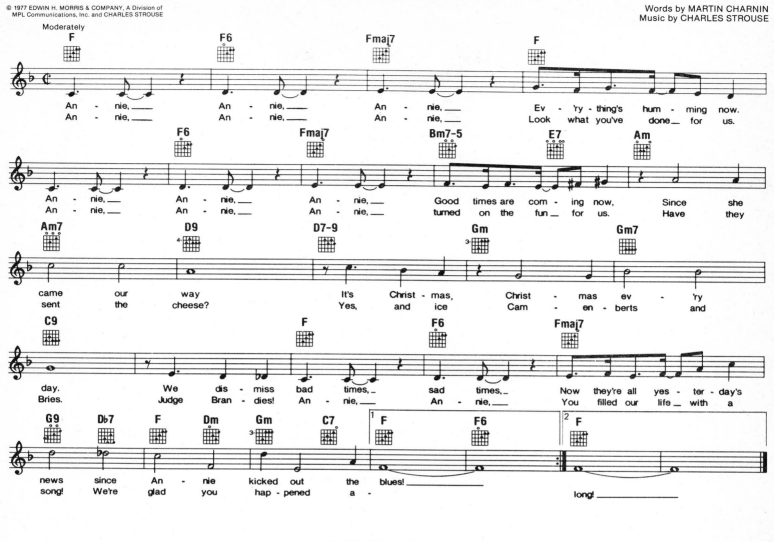

ANYWHERE I WANDER
(From "Hans Christian Andersen")

By FRANK LOESSER

ANOTHER HONKY TONK NIGHT ON BROADWAY

Words and Music by STEVE DORFF,
MILTON BROWN & SNUFF GARRETT

ANOTHER DAY

Words and Music by McCARTNEY

APPLE HONEY

By WOODY HERMAN

ANNIE DOESN'T LIVE HERE ANYMORE

Words by
JOE YOUNG & JOHNNY BURKE
Music by HAROLD SPINA

AUTUMN LEAVES

English Lyric. by JOHNNY MERCER
French Lyric by JACQUES PREVERT
Music by JOSEPH KOSMA

ARIANNE

Words and Music by CHRISTIAN ROUDEY
English Adaptation by MARTIN CHARNIN

ARROW THROUGH ME

Words and Music by
McCARTNEY

BABY, TALK TO ME
(From the Broadway Musical "Bye Bye Birdie")

Words by LEE ADAMS
Music by CHARLES STROUSE

AT THE BALLET
(From the Musical Production "A Chorus Line")

Music by MARVIN HAMLISCH
Lyric by EDWARD KLEBAN

BELLS OF WASHINGTON

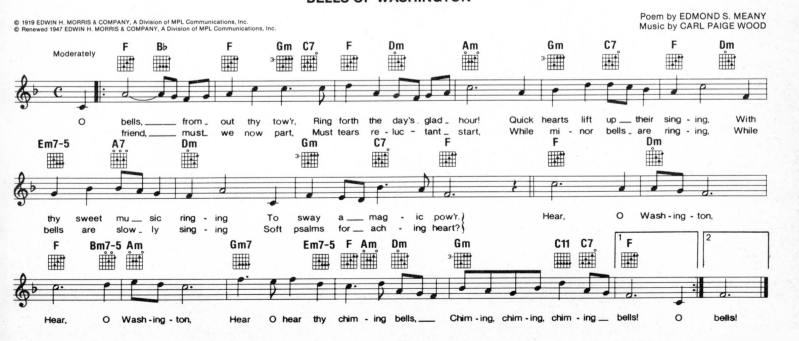

Poem by EDMOND S. MEANY
Music by CARL PAIGE WOOD

BROTHERHOOD OF MAN
(from "How To Succeed In Business Without Really Trying")

By FRANK LOESSER

There is a Broth-er-hood ____ Of Man,
mem-ber-ship ____ is free.
A ____ be-nev-o-lent Broth-er-hood ____

Of Man,
you can.
A no-ble tie that binds
Oh aren't you proud to be ____
all hu-man hearts and minds ____
in that fra-ter-ni-ty. ____

in-to one Broth-er-hood Of Man.
the great big
Your life-long
Broth-er-hood Of Man? ____

A BUSHEL AND A PECK
(From "Guys And Dolls")

By FRANK LOESSER

I love you A Bu-shel And A Peck A Bu-shel And A Peck and a hug a-round the neck Hug a-round the neck and a barrel and a heap
I love you A Bu-shel And A Peck A Bu-shel And A Peck tho' you make my heart a wreck Make my heart a wreck and you make my life a mess

Bar-rel and a heap and I'm talk-in' in my sleep a-bout } you ____ a-bout you ____ 'Cause I love you A Bu-shel And A Peck y'
Make my life a mess yes a mess of hap-pi-ness a-bout }

bet your pur-ty neck I do ____ Doo-dle oo-dle Doo-dle doo-dle oo-dle oo-dle doo-dle oo-dle oo-dle ooo. ____

BY THE LIGHT OF THE SILVERY MOON

Lyric by ED MADDEN
Music by GUS EDWARDS

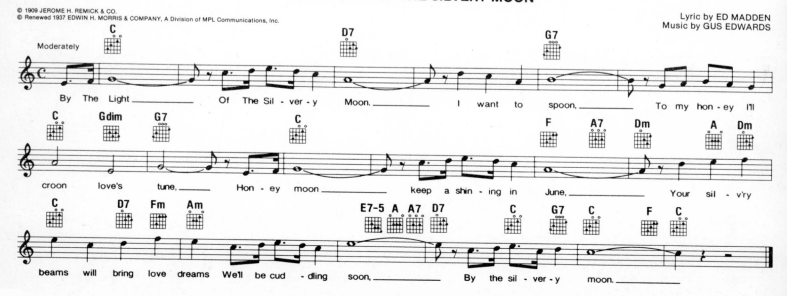

By The Light ____ Of The Sil-ver-y Moon. ____ I want to spoon, ____ To my hon-ey I'll

croon love's tune, ____ Hon-ey moon ____ keep a shin-ing in June, ____ Your sil-v'ry

beams will bring love dreams We'll be cud-dling soon, ____ By the sil-ver-y moon.

Big City Miss Ruth Ann

Words and Music by
THOMAS A. LAZAROS

Moderately Slow

BYE BYE BIRDIE
(From the Motion Picture "Bye Bye Birdie")

Words by LEE ADAMS
Music by CHARLES STROUSE

Moderately

BAND ON THE RUN

Words and Music by
McCARTNEY

3. Well the night was falling as the desert world began to settle down.
In the town they're searching for us ev'rywhere but we never will be found.
Band On The Run; Band On The Run;

And the country judge who held a grudge will search for evermore
For the Band On The Run, Band On The Run,
Band On The Run, Band On The Run.

BABY'S REQUEST

Words & Music by
McCARTNEY

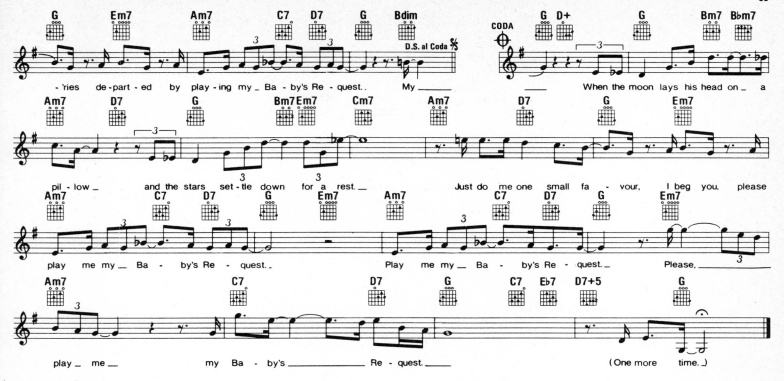

BASIN STREET BLUES

Words & Music by SPENCER WILLIAMS

BLUE EYES

Copyright © 1982 Big Pig Music Ltd.
Published in the U.S.A. by Intersong · U.S.A., Inc.

Words and Music by
ELTON JOHN and GARY OSBORNE

THE BALLAD OF THE SAD YOUNG MEN
(From "The Nervous Set")

© 1959 FRANK MUSIC CORP.

Lyric by FRAN LANDESMAN
Music by TOMMY WOLF

BEAUTY SCHOOL DROPOUT
(From the Musical Production "Grease")

Lyric & Music by
WARREN CASEY & JIM JACOBS

Bandstand Boogie

Words by
BARRY MANILOW & BRUCE SUSSMAN
Music by CHARLES ALBERTINE

BY THE TIME I GET TO PHOENIX

Words & Music by
JIM WEBB

BEFORE THE PARADE PASSES BY
(From the Musical Production "Hello, Dolly!")

Music & Lyric by
JERRY HERMAN

BEING IN LOVE
(From "The Music Man")

By MEREDITH WILLSON

THE BEST IS YET TO COME

Lyric by CAROLYN LEIGH
Music by CY COLEMAN

BELLY UP TO THE BAR, BOYS
(From "The Unsinkable Molly Brown")

By MEREDITH WILLSON

THE BLUE AND WHITE

Words by REV. CLARIS EDWIN SILCOX
Music by CLAYTON E. BUSH

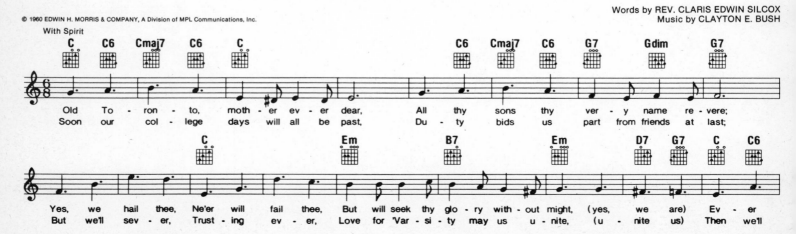

BEYOND THE SEA

Music and French Lyric by CHARLES TRENET
English Lyric by JACK LAWRENCE

The Best Thing You've Ever Done

Lyric & Music by
MARTIN CHARNIN

BUGLE CALL RAG

Lyric and Music by
JACK PETTIS, BILLY MEYERS
& ELMER SCHOEBEL

BIG D
(From "The Most Happy Fella")

By FRANK LOESSER

BLESSED ARE THE BELIEVERS

Words & Music by
RORY BOURKE, CHARLIE BLACK,
& SANDY PINKARD

BIG GIRLS DON'T CRY

Words & Music by
BOB CREWE & BOB GAUDIO

BLUE, TURNING GREY OVER YOU

Words by ANDY RAZAF
Music by THOMAS WALLER

BLUEBIRD

Words & Music by
McCARTNEY

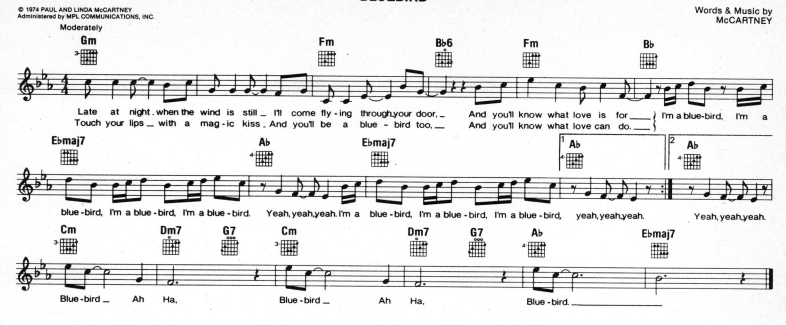

Late at night. when the wind is still _ I'll come fly-ing through your door, _ And you'll know what love is for ____ } I'm a blue-bird, I'm a
Touch your lips _ with a mag-ic kiss. And you'll be a blue - bird too, _ And you'll know what love can do. _

blue-bird, I'm a blue-bird, I'm a blue-bird. Yeah, yeah, yeah. I'm a blue-bird, I'm a blue-bird, I'm a blue-bird, yeah, yeah, yeah. Yeah, yeah, yeah.

Blue-bird _ Ah Ha, Blue-bird _ Ah Ha, Blue-bird. _____

BORN TOO LATE

Words by FRED TOBIAS
Music by CHARLES STROUSE

Born Too Late for you to no-tice me, To you I'm just a kid that you won't date, Why was I Born Too

Late? _____ Born Too Late to have a chance to win your love, Oh why, oh why was

it my fate to be Born Too Late? _____ I see you walk with an-oth-er, I

wish it could be me; I long to hold you and kiss you, But I know it nev-er can be. For I was Born Too Late for

you to care, Now my heart cries be cause your heart just could - n't wait, Why was I Born To Late?

Why was I Born Too Late? _____ Why was I Born Too Late? _____

BLUE FLAME

Lyric by LEO CORDAY
Music by JAMES NOBLE & JOE BISHOP

BOO-HOO

By EDWARD HEYMAN,
CARMEN LOMBARDO & JOHN JACOB LOEB

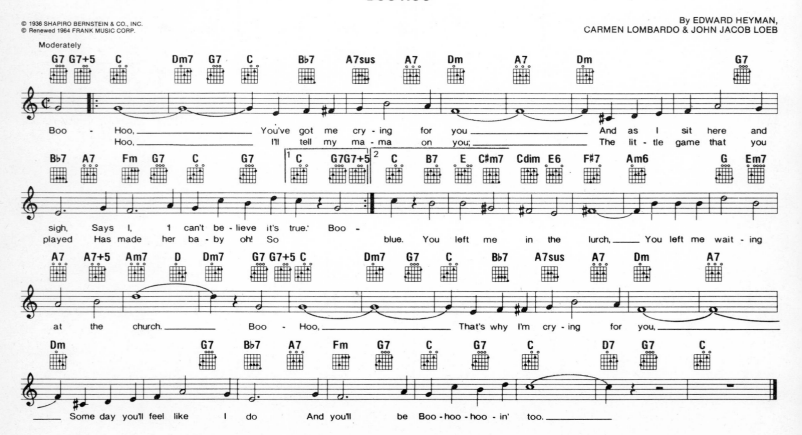

BORN TO BE WITH YOU

Words & Music by
DON ROBERTSON

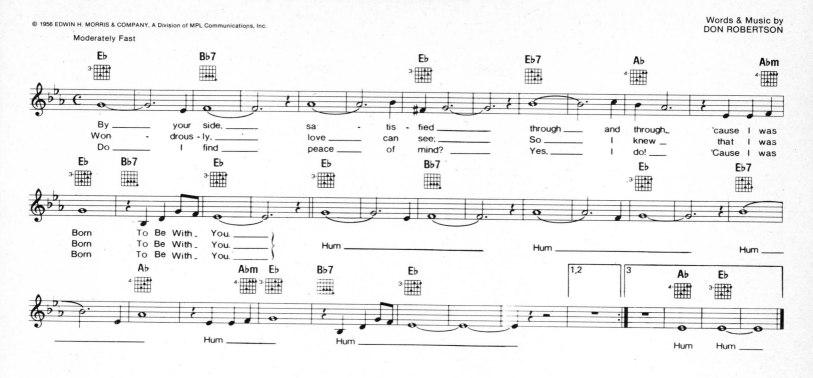

BALLROOM DANCING

Words and Music by
McCARTNEY

(THE ORIGINAL)
Boogie Woogie

By CLARENCE "PINE TOP" SMITH

THE BUCKEYE BATTLE CRY

By FRANK CRUMIT

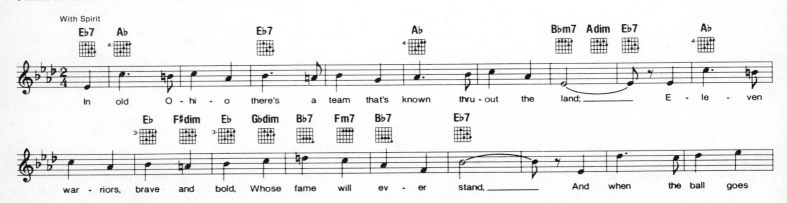

o - ver,_____ Our cheers will reach the sky,_____ O - hi - o field will hear a -

gain the _ Buck - eye Bat - tle Cry,_____ Drive, drive on down the field,_____

Men of the scar - let and grey;_____ Don't let them thru that line,_____ We have to win this

game to - day, Come on Ohio, Smash thru to vic - to - ry,_____ We cheer you as we

go;_____ Our _ hon - or de - fend, So, we'll fight to the end for O - hi - o._____

BROKEN-HEARTED MELODY

Words by HAL DAVID
Music by SHERMAN EDWARDS

VERSE

Bro - ken - Heart - ed Mel - o - dy,_____ Once _____ you were our

song of love.._____ Now _____ you just keep taunt - ing me!_____ With _____

_____ the mem-o-ry of {his - a / her - a} ten - der love. Oh! Bro - ken-Heart - ed Mel - o - dy,_ Must you keep re -
Bro - ken-Heart - ed Mel - o - dy,_ Won't you bring {him / her}

mind - ing me,_ Of the lips I long to kiss And the love I miss, Since {he / she} went a - way,_____
back to me? Sing to {him / her} un - til {he / she} yearns,_ For when {he / she} re - turns, No more will you

Night and day they play. That be _____ A Bro - ken - Heart - ed Mel - o - dy!_____

BABY, IT'S COLD OUTSIDE
(From "Neptune's Daughter")

By FRANK LOESSER

BRONCO BILLY

Words and Music by MILTON L. BROWN,
SNUFF GARRETT & STEPHEN H. DORFF

THE BEST IN THE WORLD
(From "A Day In Hollywood")

Music and Lyric by
JERRY HERMAN

Here's the way that my sto-ry goes _ at the old Cin-nin-nat-i Loew's _ I was work-in' from five to mid-night as an ush-er-
(Said good-bye to the) beat up Loew's, hitched my way to the stu-di-os. _ Know-ing this lit-tle la-dy would be con-quer-ing the

ette. "You're too good to be hold-ing doors,"Pa-pa said, "With a face like yours _ there's a for-tune out there that you just got-ta go and
west. Thru the lean and the hun-gry days _ liv-ing most-ly on Pa-pa's praise till I heard some-one whis-per, "Why not give the girl a

get." I put a-way my flash-light and my gloves to go and be the star the whole world loves. Pa-pa said, "You're the
test?" My knees were shak-ing and my hands were cold. But I re-mem-ber as the cam-'ras rolled. _

best, _ you're the best in the world. All you need is the chance to be best in the world. You're the bright lit-tle star _ that stands out from the
You're the best in the world. All you need is the chance to be best in the world. You're the bright lit-tle star _ that stands out from the

rest. If you make it or not, don't for-get what you've got, Pa-pa said you're the best." Said good-bye to the
rest. If you make it or not, don't for-get what you've got, Pa-pa said you're the best. I was mold-ed and all. Life can have its i-

best! _ I'm the best in the world, I'm the best in the world. I'm the bright lit-tle star _ that stands out from the
rest. If I make it or not, don't for-get what I've got, it's been drummed in my head, Pa-pa said, Pa-pa said, Pa-pa said I'm the best!" _

3. (I was molded and) redesigned
and expensively wined and dined.
I was living a life I'd just imagined in my heart.
I was given the grand approach,
started work with an acting coach
and in no time at all they handed me a leading part.
I know that Papa's dream was awf'ly near.
So, guess who flew out for the big premiere.
In the hush and the (To Coda)

4. (Life can have its i -)ronic ways
for the picture ran seven days.
And disconsolate back to Cincinnati Papa went.
Even tho' a few dreams were dashed,
more than one little hope was crashed,
but you shrug and you say,"A girl has gotta pay her rent."
Usher wanted read the Sunday ad.
They asked me what experience I had.
"Sir," I said, "I'm the (To Coda)

CAN'T YOU JUST SEE YOURSELF?
(From the Broadway Musical "High Button Shoes")

Lyric by SAMMY CAHN
Music by JULE STYNE

CANDIDA

Words & Music by
TONI WINE & IRWIN LEVINE

CALDONIA
(What Makes Your Big Head So Hard?)

Words & Music by
FLEECIE MOORE

Medium Boogie Woogie Tempo

Walk-in' with mah ba-by, she's got great big feet, She's long, lean and lan-ky, ain't had noth-in' to eat, But she's my ba-by __ And I

love her __ just the same. _____ Cra-zy 'bout that wo-man 'cause Cal-don-ia is __ her name. _____

Cal-don-ia! __ Cal-don-ia! __ What Makes Your Big Head So Hard? But I love you, __

love you __ just __ the same. _____ Cra-zy 'bout that wo-man 'cause Cal-don-ia is __ her name. _____

Cal-don-ia! __ Cal-don-ia! __ What Makes Your Big Head So Hard?

CAPTAIN HOOK'S WALTZ
(From the Musical Production "Peter Pan")

Lyric by
BETTY COMDEN & ADOLPH GREEN
Music by JULE STYNE

Moderately, with a lilt

Who's the swin-i-est swine in the world? Cap-tain Hook. __ Cap-tain Hook. __ Who's the

dirt-i-est dog in this won-der-ful world? Cap-tain Hook. __ Cap-tain Hook. __ Cap-tain of

vil-lain-y, mur-der and loot. __ Ea-ger to kill an-y who

say that my hook is-n't cute. Who's the slim-i-est rat in the pack? __ Cap-tain Hook. __ Cap-tain Hook. __
creep-i-est creep in the world? __ Cap-tain Hook. __ Cap-tain Hook. __

COLD, COLD HEART

Words and Music by
HANK WILLIAMS

CANDY GIRL

Words & Music by
LARRY SANTOS

COMME CI, COMME CA

English Words by JOAN WHITNEY & ALEX KRAMER
French Words by PIERRE DUDAN
Music by BRUNO COQUATRIX

CARELESS HANDS

Words & Music by
BOB HILLIARD & CARL SIGMAN

CARPET MAN

Words & Music by
JIM WEBB

CASA LOMA STOMP

By H. EUGENE GIFFORD

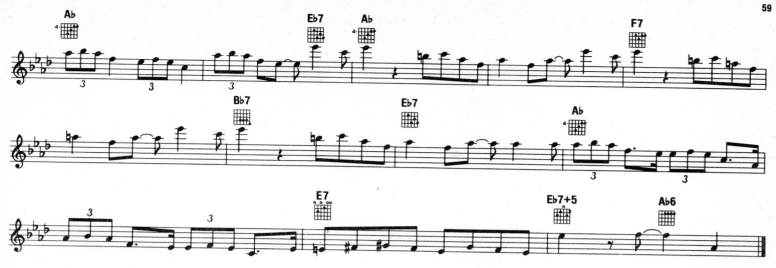

CHRISTOPHER COLUMBUS

Words by ANDY RAZAF
Music by LEON BERRY

Mis- ter Chris- to- pher Co- lum- bus, __ Sailed the sea with- out a com-
Mis- ter Chris- to- pher Co- lum- bus, __ He used rhy- thm as a com-

- pass; __ When his men be- gan a rum- pus, __
- pass, __ Mu- sic end- ed all the rum- pus, __

Up spoke, Chris- to- pher Co- lum- bus: __ There is land __ some- where, un- til we __
Wise old Chris- to- pher Co- lum- bus, __ Since the world is round, we'll be safe, __

get there, __ We will not __ go wrong, __ If we sing, __ 'swing a song:
and sound, __ Till our goal __ is found, __ We'll just keep, __ rhy- thm bound:

Soon the crew was mak- in' __ mer- ry, __ Then came a yell, __

__ 'Let's drink __ to Is- a- belle, Hum, bring the rum, Ho, Hum! No more mu- ti- ny, __

what a time __ at sea, __ With di- plo- ma- cy, __ Chris- ty made his- to- ry. __

CECILIA
(Does Your Mother Know You're Out)

Words by HERMAN RUBY
Music by DAVE DREYER

Does your moth-er know you're out Ce-ci-lia? Does she know that I'm a-bout to steal

you, Oh, my, when I look in your eyes __ Some-thing tells me

you and I should get to-geth-er, How a-bout a lit-tle kiss Ce-ci-lia,

Just a kiss you'll nev-er miss Ce-ci-lia, Why do we two keep on wast-ing

time, Oh, Ce-ci-lia, say that you'll be mine. _____ mine. _____

CHOO CHOO CH'BOOGIE

Words & Music by
VAUGHN HORTON, DENVER DARLING
& MILTON GABLER

I'm head-in' for the sta-tion with my pack on my back, __ I'm tired of trans-port-a-tion in the back of a hack, I
gon-na set-tle down be-side the rail-road track,___ And live the life o' Ri-ley in a beat-en down shack, So

love to hear the rhy-thm of the click-e-ty clack, __ And hear the lone-some whis-tle, See the smoke from the stack, __ And
when I hear a whis-tle I can peep thru the crack, __ And watch the train a-roll-in when it's ball-in-the-jack, __ For

pal a-round with dem-o-crat-ic fel-lows named "Mac" __ So, take me right back to the track, Jack!
I just love the rhy-thm of the click-e-ty clack, __ So take me right back to the track, Jack!

Choo-Choo __ Choo-Choo Ch-Boo-gie, Woo-Woo __ Boo-gie Woo-gie, Choo-Choo, __

Choo-Choo Ch'Boo-gie; Take me right back to the track, Jack! I'm Take me right back to the track, Jack!

CHILDREN CHILDREN

Words & Music by
McCARTNEY-LAINE

CRYING MY HEART OUT OVER YOU

Words and Music by CARL BUTLER,
MARIJOHN WILKIN, LOUISE CERTAIN & GLADYS STACEY

CHRISTMAS IS A-COMIN'
(May God Bless You)

Words & Music by
FRANK LUTHER

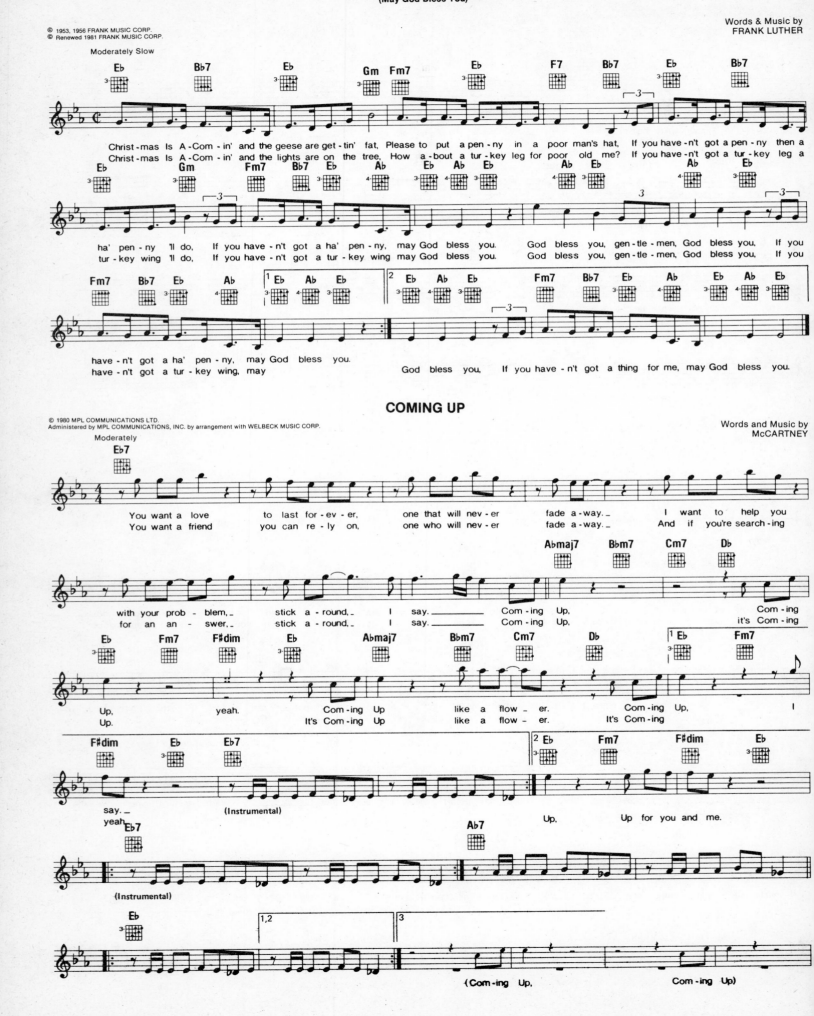

COMING UP

Words and Music by
McCARTNEY

It's Com-ing Up, it's Com-ing Up, I say._ It's Com-ing Up like a flow _ er, it's Com-ing Up. I feel it in my bones You want a bet-ter kind of fu-ture. One that ev-'ry-one can share_ You're not a-lone, we all could use it. Stick a-round, we're near-ly there._ It's Com-ing Up, it's Com-ing Up ev-'ry where._ It's Com-ing Up like a flow _ er. It's Com-ing Up for all to share. It's Com-ing Up, yeah. It's Com-ing Up an-y-way. It's Com-ng Up like a flow-er. Com-ing Up. _____

CIVILIZATION
(Bongo, Bongo, Bongo)
(From the Broadway Musical "Angel In The Wings")

By BOB HILLIARD
& CARL SIGMAN

Medium Swing

Bon-go, Bon-go, Bon-go, I don't want to leave the Con-go, Oh, no, no, no, no, no!_____ Bin-gle, ban-gle, bun-gle, I'm so hap-py in the jun-gle I re-fuse to go. _____ Don't want no bright lights, false teeth, door-bells, land-lords, I make it clear _____ That, no mat-ter how they coax me, I'll stay right here! _____ They have things like the a-tom bomb, So, I think I'll stay where I 'om'._ Civ-i-li-za-tion, I'll stay right here! _____

THE CHRISTMAS SONG
(Chestnuts Roasting On An Open Fire)

Words & Music by
MEL TORME & ROBERT WELLS

Moderately

Chest-nuts roast-ing on an op-en fire, Jack Frost nip-ping at your nose, Yule-tide car-ols be-ing

sung by a choir And folks dressed up like Es-ki-mos. Ev-'ry-bo-dy knows a tur-key and some mis-tle-toe ___

Help to make the sea-son bright. Ti-ny tots with their eyes all a-glow Will find it hard to sleep to-night. They know that

San - ta's on his way; He's load-ed lots of toys and good-ies on his sleigh And ev-'ry moth-er's child ___ is gon-na

spy ___ To see if rein-deer ___ real-ly know how to fly. And so, I'm of-fer-ing this sim-ple phrase To

kids from one to nine-ty-two. Al-tho' it's been said ma-ny times, ma-ny ways; 'Mer-ry Christ-mas to you.'

COPENHAGEN

Words by WALTER MELROSE
Music by CHARLIE DAVIS

Moderately

Pro - fess-er man won't you play Cop-en-hag-en ___ 'cause that's one tune _ sure has got me run-nin'
Pro - fess-er man won't you play Cop-en-hag-en ___ 'cause that's the tune _ drives my danc-in' shoes in

wild _____ No - bod-y knows how that tune burns up my clothes So
sane _____ Be good to me jazz me with that mel-o-dy ___ So

Hey Hey Hey ___ Syn-co-pate it all night long. _____ Doo da da
Hey Hey Hey ___ Syn-co-pate it all night long. _____

Fine

D.C. al Fine

doo dum Step-pin dad-dy ___ mammas' feel-in ___ good ___ should ___
Syn-co-pate me _ like a dad-dy ___

COUNT EVERY STAR

Words by SAMMY GALLOP
Music by BRUNO COQUATRIX

CRUISING DOWN THE RIVER

Words & Music by
EILY BEADELL & NELL TOLLERTON

COCOANUT SWEET
(From the Musical Production "Jamaica")

Lyric by E.Y. HARBURG
Music by HAROLD ARLEN

CONNIE-O

Words & Music by
BOB CREWE & BOB GAUDIO

COOK OF THE HOUSE

Words & Music by
McCARTNEY

COMING IN AND OUT OF YOUR LIFE

Words and Music by
RICHARD PARKER & BOBBY WHITESIDE

CAFÉ ON THE LEFT BANK

Words & Music by
McCARTNEY

CAROLINA MOON

Words & Music by
BENNY DAVIS & JOE BURKE

CHARLOTTE'S WEB

Words and Music by JOHN DURRILL,
CLIFF CROFFORD & SNUFF GARRETT

Spend the night in Char-lotte's bed _ you might get caught _ in Char-lotte's Web
Char-lotte took me late one night _ to a se-cret room by can-dle light

grow-in' wild _ Char-lotte holds _ more se-crets than the Nile _ She spins and weaves her ma-gic spell _ Her
read my hand and said she hoped _ that I would un-der-stand _ She turned two cards up face to face _ She

bo-dy speaks _ what words can't tell I'm the moth _ she's the flame _ In a town that's all _ too quick to smear her
said two hearts _ have found their place Now all the rest is his-to-ry _ The fu-ture's full _ of Char-lotte lov-in'

name _ But I'll } take the likes of Char-lotte and _ her kind. _ Small town talk don't mat-ter now _ that
me _ And I'll }

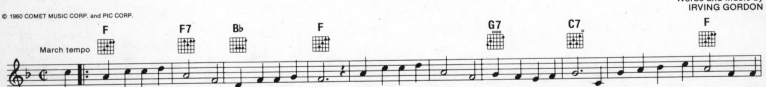

Char-lotte's mine It may be true that o-ther men _ have found _ her bed. _ But I'm the one who's caught in Char-lotte's

1. F6 Web
2. F Web It
D.S. al Coda

CODA F Web Char-lotte's Web
Repeat and Fade

DELAWARE

Words and Music by
IRVING GORDON

March tempo

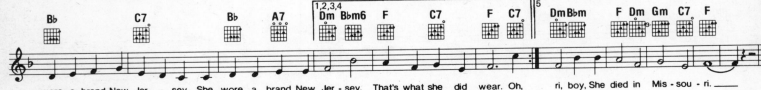

Oh, What did Del-la wear, boy? What did Del-la wear? What did Del-la wear, boy? What did Del-la wear? She wore a brand New Jer-sey, She
Why did Cal-i-phone-ya? Why did Cal-i-phone-ya? Why did Cal-i-phone-ya? Was she all a-lone? She called to say Ha-wai-a, She

1,2,3,4   5
wore a brand New Jer - sey, She wore a brand New Jer - sey, That's what she did wear. Oh,   ri, boy, She died in Mis-sou-ri. _
called to say Ha-wai - a, She called to say Ha-wai - a, That's why she did phone. Oh,

3. What did Mis-sis-sip, boy? What did Mis-sis-sip?
What did Mis-sis-sip, boy? Thro' her pretty lip?
She sipped a Min-ne-so-ta, She sipped a Min-ne-so-ta,
She sipped a Min-ne-so-ta, That's what she did sip.

4. Where has Or-e-gon, boy? Where has Or-e-gon?
If you want A-las-ka, A-las-ka where she's gone.
She went to pay her Tex-as, She went to pay her Tex-as,
She went to pay her Tex-as, That's where she has gone.

5. How did Wis-con-sin, boy? She stole a New-brass-key,
Too bad that Ar-kan-saw, And so did Ten-nes-see.
It made poor Flo-ra-die, boy, It made poor Flo-ra-die,
You see she died in Mis-sou-ri, boy, She died in Mis-sou-ri.

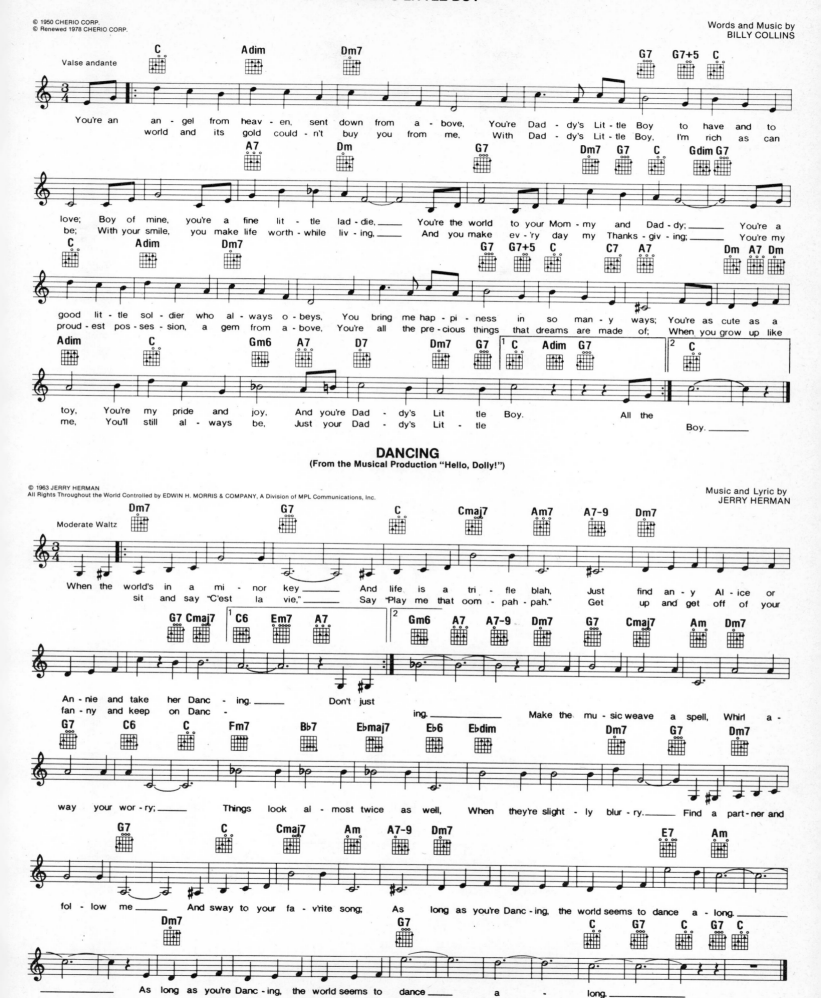

DADDY'S LITTLE GIRL

Words and Music by
BOBBY BURKE & HORACE GERLACH

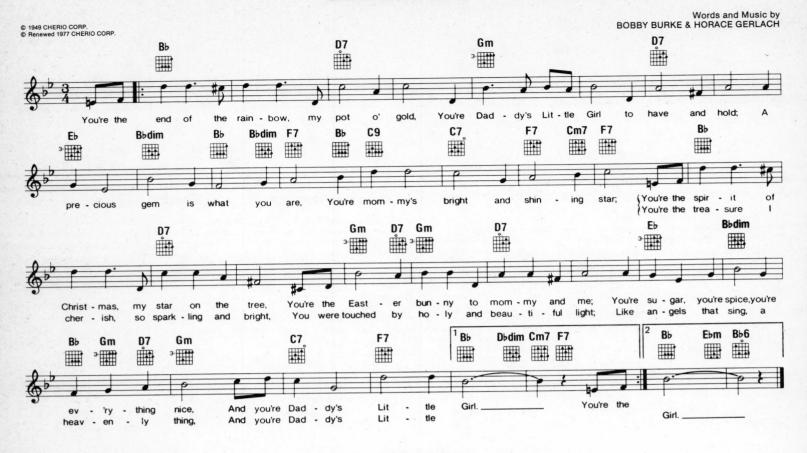

You're the end of the rain-bow, my pot o' gold, You're Dad-dy's Lit-tle Girl to have and hold; A

pre-cious gem is what you are, You're mom-my's bright and shin-ing star; You're the spir-it of
You're the trea-sure I

Christ-mas, my star on the tree, You're the East-er bun-ny to mom-my and me; You're su-gar, you're spice, you're
cher-ish, so spark-ling and bright, You were touched by ho-ly and beau-ti-ful light; Like an-gels that sing, a

ev-'ry-thing nice, And you're Dad-dy's Lit-tle Girl. You're the
heav-en-ly thing, And you're Dad-dy's Lit-tle Girl. Girl.

DANCE: TEN; LOOKS: THREE
(From the Musical Production "A Chorus Line")

Music by MARVIN HAMLISCH
Lyric by EDWARD KLEBAN

Moderately

Dance: Ten; Looks: Three, and I'm still on un-em-ploy-ment, danc-ing for my own en-joy-ment.
Flat and sas-sy, I would get the strays an los-ers. Beg-gars real-ly can't be choos-ers.

That ain't it, kid! That ain't it, kid! Dance: Ten; Looks: Three is like to die. Left the the-'ter and
That ain't it, kid! That ain't it, kid! Fix the chas-sis, "How do you do!" Life turned in to an

called the doc-tor for my ap-point-ment to buy tits and ass. Bought my-self a
end-less med-ley of "Gee, it had to be you." Why? Tits and ass. Where the cup-board

fan-cy pair, Tight-ened up the der-ri-ere. Did the nose with it, all that goes with it. Tits and ass!
once was bare, Now you knock and some-one's there. You have got 'em, hey! Top to bot-tom, hey! It's a gas!

Had the bin-go-bon-gos done. Sud-den-ly I'm get-ting Nash. 'nal tours! Tits and
Just a dash of sil-i-cone. Shake your new ma-ra-cas and you're fine! Tits and

DINAH

Words by SAM M. LEWIS and JOE YOUNG
Music by HARRY AKST

74

DON'T LET THE SUN GO DOWN ON ME

Words and Music by
ELTON JOHN & BERNIE TAUPIN

Dear Boy

Words and Music by
McCARTNEY

DEAR OLD NEBRASKA U.
(There Is No Place Like Nebraska)

Words and Music by HARRY PECHA

DAYTIME NIGHTIME SUFFERING

Words and Music by
McCARTNEY

DEAR WORLD
(From the Broadway Musical "Dear World")

Music and Lyric by
JERRY HERMAN

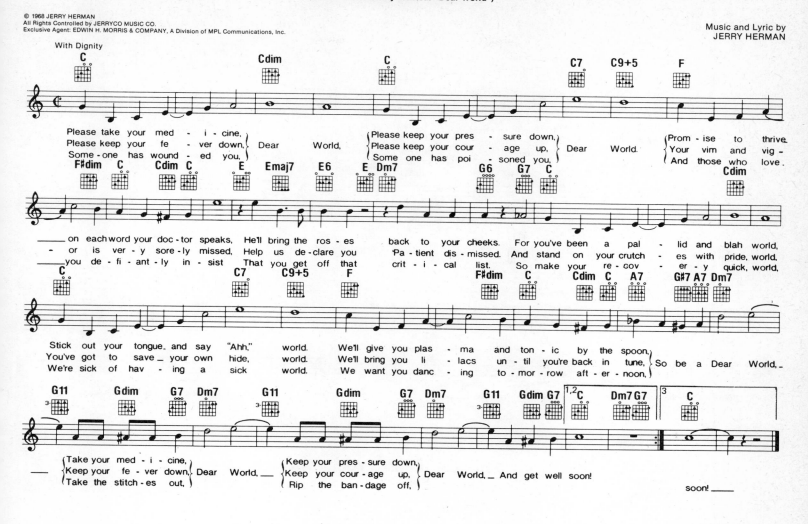

DADDY SANG BASS

Words and Music by
CARL PERKINS

DISTANT MELODY
(From "Peter Pan")

Lyric by BETTY COMDEN and ADOLPH GREEN
Music by JULE STYNE

DON'T LET IT BRING YOU DOWN

Words and Music by
McCARTNEY-LAINE

DOCTOR JAZZ

Lyric by WALTER MELROSE
Music by JOSEPH OLIVER

DETROIT CITY

Words and Music by
DANNY DILL & MELL TILLIS

Recitation

Cause you know I rode a freight train north to Detroit City.
And after all these years I find I've just been wasting my time,
So I just think I'll take my foolish pride and put it on the south-bound freight and ride
And go on back to the loved ones, the ones that I left waiting so far behind,
I wanna go home, I wanna go home; Oh, how I wanna go home.

DON'T LIKE GOODBYES
(From "HOUSE OF FLOWERS")

Lyric by TRUMAN CAPOTE and HAROLD ARLEN
Music by HAROLD ARLEN

(Doop Doo-De-Oop)
A DOODLIN' SONG

Lyric by CAROLYN LEIGH
Music by CY COLEMAN

DOWN THE LINE

© 1926 UNIVERSITY OF NOTRE DAME
© Renewed 1954 UNIVERSITY OF NOTRE DAME
All Rights Controlled by EDWIN H. MORRIS & COMPANY, A Division of MPL Communications, Inc.

Words by VINCENT F. FAGEN
Music by JOSEPH J. CASASANTA

DRIFTING AND DREAMING
(Sweet Paradise)

© 1925 EDWIN H. MORRIS & COMPANY, A Division of MPL Communications, Inc.
© Renewed 1953 EDWIN H. MORRIS & COMPANY, A Division of MPL Communications, Inc.

Lyric by HAVEN GILLESPIE
Music by EGBERT VAN ALSTYNE,
ERWIN R. SCHMIDT and LOYAL CURTIS

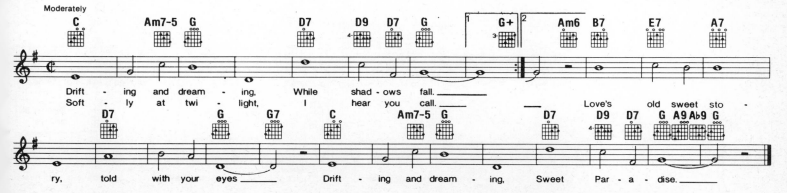

DOODLE DOO DOO

© 1924 LEO FEIST, INC.
© Renewed 1952 EDWIN H. MORRIS & COMPANY, A Division of MPL Communications, Inc.

Words and Music by
ART KASSELL & MEL STITZEL

DON'T GO BREAKING MY HEART

Copyright © 1976 by Big Pig Music Ltd.
Subpublished in the U.S.A. by Intersong-USA, Inc.

Words and Music by
CARTE BLANCHE & ANN ORSON

DON'T COME KNOCKIN'

Words and Music by
MICHAEL P. HEENEY & FRANCY MATAN

Moderately Fast

Verse

We been in love and we been out. _
You ain't pickin' me up just to put me _ down._
Loved e-nough to know what it's a-bout._
No more leavin' my heart spinnin' 'round and 'round. _

It took a hurt to let me know_ you were playin' touch and go. So why you knock-in' at my door a-gain?_ Well, I'm not
Nev-er knowin' where it's gonna stop,_ at the bottom or_ the top. So bab - y, Don't Come Knock'n at my heart._ You best stop

Chorus

_____gon-na let _you back in. Don't Come Knock'n at my door._ Your love don't live here any-more. _ Don't go door bell ringin' and love_
be-fore _ you start.

_____ song sing-in'. We both been there be-fore. _ Don't come tryin' to find my heart. It's still in pieces _ and parts _

1. Em A D
2. Em A D

D.S. and Fade

from when you came 'round be-fore _____ knock'n at my _ door. _
Don't come

EASY RIDER
(I Wonder Where My Easy Rider's Gone)

By SHELTON BROOKS

Moderately

I won-der where_ my Eas-y Rid-er's gone to - day,_
won-der where_ my Eas-y Rid-er's gone, Dog - gone!_
He nev - er told me he was goin a - way;_
He went and put my brand new watch in pawn;_

If he was here, he'd win the race,_ If not first, he'd get a "place,"_ Cash in our tick-ets for a
He had those fasc-in-a-tin' eyes,_ That just seem to hip-no-tize,_ I'm sigh-ing for - and I am

jol-ly "joy-ride" right a - way. _ I'm los-in' all _ my mon-ey, that is why I'm blue,_ To
cry-ing for that lov-in' man. _ I've got the blues,_ but I am too darn mean to cry,_ He'll

win a race, he knows just what to do;_ I'd put all my junk in pawn,_ To bet on an-y horse that Joc-key's
come a limp-in' home-ward bye and bye;_ Oh, tell me now have you seen _ My hand-some ev-er-lov-in' Sam-my

1. Bb G#dim F7 F+
2. Bb Ebm Bb F7 Bb

on, _ Oh! I won-der where my Eas-y Rid-er's gone. _
Green, _ Oh! I won-der where my Eas-y Rid-er's gone. _

84

EASY STREET
(From the Musical Production "Annie")

Lyric by MARTIN CHARNIN
Music by CHARLES STROUSE

ELEGANCE
(From the Musical Production "Hello, Dolly!")

Music and Lyric by
JERRY HERMAN

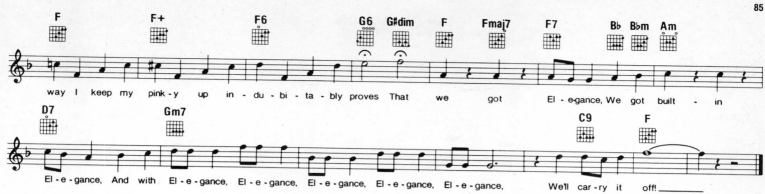

way I keep my pink-y up in-du-bi-ta-bly proves That we got El-e-gance, We got built-in El-e-gance, And with El-e-gance, El-e-gance, El-e-gance, El-e-gance, El-e-gance, We'll car-ry it off!

EVERY WHICH WAY BUT LOOSE

Words and Music by STEPHEN DORFF,
MILTON BROWN & SNUFF GARRETT

Medium Country

I've al-ways been the kind of man who does-n't be-lieve in strings long term ob-li-ga-tions are just un-ne-ces-sar-y things But girl you've got me think-in' while I'm drink-in' one more beer If I'm head-ed for a heart-ache then why the hell am I still here I'm test-ing my re-sis-tance and it's

comes up in the mor-nin' it should wear-in' might-y thin I've got the feel-ing I should leave be-fore the roof caves in My find me some-place new But right this min-ute all I want is to lay here next to you Those

mind tells me to move a-long but my bo-dy begs me "stay. and now I feel the need to hold you close and mem-o-ries still keep call-in' me from some-where in my past Bet-ter hur-ry if they want me cause I can

love the night a-way } While you're turn-ing me Eve-ry Which Way But Loose You turn me feel me fad-ing fast }

Eve-ry Which Way But Loose In-side the fi-re's burn-ing me In my mind you just keep turn-ing me Eve-ry Which Way But Loose

Ba-by there's no ex-cuse you turn me Eve-ry Which Way But Loose When the sun Loose

EMPTY GARDEN
(Hey Hey Johnny)

Words and Music by
ELTON JOHN & BERNIE TAUPIN

EBONY AND IVORY

Words and Music by
McCARTNEY

EASY LOVE

Words and Music by LARRY HERBSTRITT, STEVE DORFF & RANDY CATE

LOVE THEME FROM "EYES OF LAURA MARS"
(Prisoner)

Words and Music by KAREN LAWRENCE and JOHN DESAUTELS

ENJOY YOURSELF
(It's Later Than You Think)

Lyric by HERB MAGIDSON
Music by CARL SIGMAN

FIVE MINUTES MORE

Lyric by SAMMY CAHN
Music by JULE STYNE

THE ENTERTAINER

By SCOTT JOPLIN

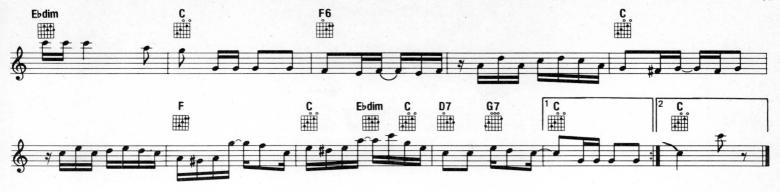

FACE IT, GIRL, IT'S OVER

Words and Music by
FRANK H. STANTON and ANDY BADALE

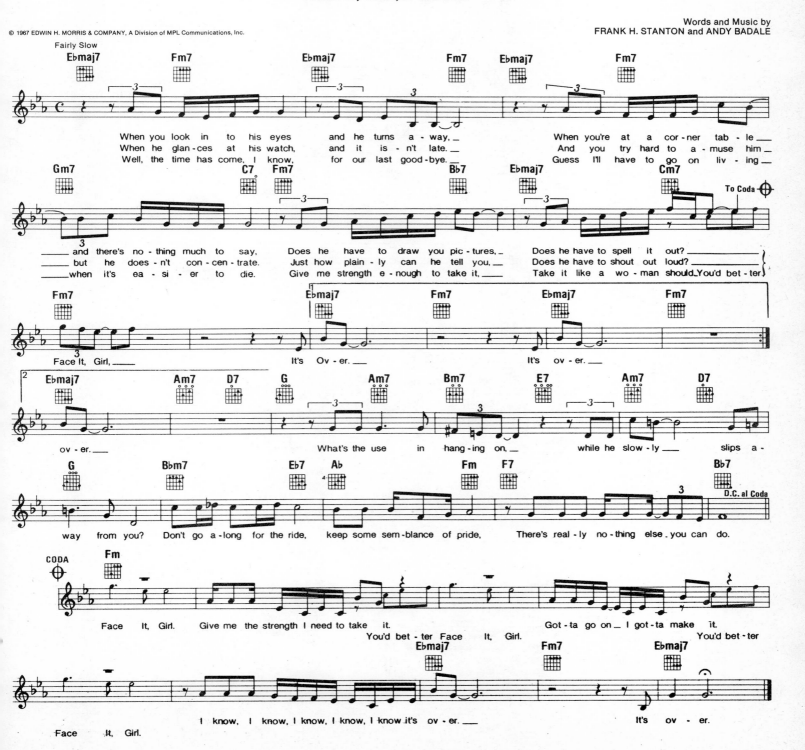

ENDLESS LOVE

Words and Music by
LIONEL RICHIE

FAR ABOVE CAYUGA'S WATERS

By C. URGUHART

Far A-bove Cay-u-ga's Wa-ters, With its waves of blue;

Stands our no-ble Al-ma Ma-ter, Glo-ri-ous to view

Lift the cho-rus, speed it on-ward, Loud her prais-es tell;

Hail to thee, our Al-ma Ma-ter! Hail, all hail, Cor-nell.

FIVE FOOT TWO, EYES OF BLUE
(Has Anybody Seen My Girl?)

Words by JOE YOUNG & SAM LEWIS
Music by RAY HENDERSON

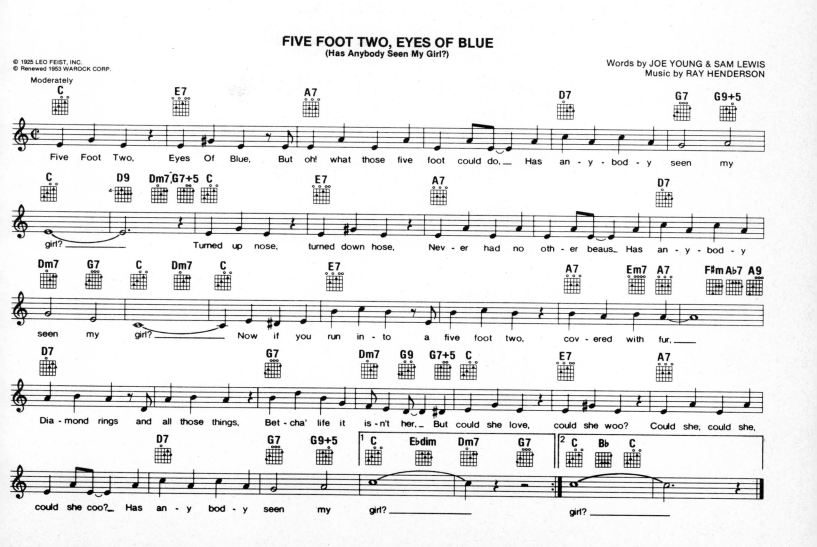

Five Foot Two, Eyes Of Blue, But oh! what those five foot could do,— Has an-y-bod-y seen my

girl? Turned up nose, turned down hose, Nev-er had no oth-er beaus. Has an-y-bod-y

seen my girl? Now if you run in-to a five foot two, cov-ered with fur,

Dia-mond rings and all those things, Bet-cha' life it is-n't her,— But could she love, could she woo? Could she, could she,

could she coo? Has an-y bod-y seen my girl? girl?

FAMOUS GROUPIES

Words and Music by
McCARTNEY

FIGHT ON

By MILO SWEET
and GLEN GRANT

Flamingo

Lyric by ED ANDERSON
Music by TED GROUYA

FOR EVERY MAN THERE'S A WOMAN
(From the Motion Picture "Casbah")

Lyric by LEO ROBIN
Music by HAROLD ARLEN

FUGUE FOR TINHORNS
(From "Guys And Dolls")

By FRANK LOESSER

FREEDOM
(From the Musical Production "Shenandoah")

Lyric by PETER UDELL
Music by GARY GELD

Baa-baa-baa-baa Baa-baa. Free-dom's in the state___ of mind. You can't get to free-dom by rid-in' on a train.___ The on-ly way to free-dom is right on through your brain,___ Wo-wo-wo___ wo-wo. Free-dom is a no-tion sweep-in' the na-tion, Free-dom is the right of all man-kind. Free-dom is a bod-y's 'mag-i-na-tion, Free-dom's in the state of mind. Free-dom, free-dom. Free-dom, free-dom. Free-dom is a no-tion sweep-in' the na-tion, Free-dom is a bod-y's 'mag-i-na-tion, Free-dom is a full time oc-cu-pa-tion, Free-dom's in the state___ of mind!___

FROM THE LAND OF THE SKY-BLUE WATER

Lyric by NELLE RICHMOND EBERHART
Music by CHARLES WAKEFIELD CADMAN

From the Land of the Sky-blue Wa-ter,___ They brought a cap-tive maid;___ And her eyes they are lit___ with light-nings___ Her heart is not___ a-fraid!___ But I steal to her lodge___ at dawn-ing,___ I woo her with___ my flute;___ She is sick for the Sky-blue Wa-ter.___ The cap-tive maid___ is mute.___

FREDDY, MY LOVE
(From the Musical Production "Grease")

Lyric and Music by WARREN CASEY and JIM JACO[...]

FALLEN ANGEL

Copyright © 1960 by CEDARWOOD PUBLISHING CO., INC., Nashville, TN

Words and Music by WAYNE P. WALKER,
WEBB PIERCE & MARIJOHN WILKIN

Last night I saw an an-gel the one I once called mine The hand that wore my wed-ding band held a glass of
man-y times she told me she could-n't take much more So man-y times I laughed at her and walked right out the

wine I took her love for grant-ed I wronged her night and day I drove my an-gel from me and
door I was-n't wor-thy of her and now my an-gel's gone The de-vil took her from me and

now she's gone a-stray She's just a Fal-len An-gel but I don't blame her for it all She's just a
claimed her for his own

Fall-en An-gel and I'm the fool who made her fall So fall

FOUR BROTHERS

© 1948, 1949 EDWIN H. MORRIS & COMPANY, A Division of MPL Communications, Inc.
© Renewed 1976, 1977 EDWIN H. MORRIS & COMPANY, A Division of MPL Communications, Inc.

By JIMMIE GIUFFRE

FIREFLY

Lyric by CAROLYN LEIGH
Music by CY COLEMAN

I call her Fi-re-fly __ 'cause oh my she ra-di-ates moon-glow __ Wants none __ of that noon-glow __ She starts to glit-ter when the sun goes down 'bout eight P. M. __ It's may-hem she switch-es those brights up __ lights up and gives me a call __ "Hey, take me to the fi-re-flies' ball!" But when I get her there, set her there, do I get to pet her there, 'n grab __ me some glow? No, she's a gad-a-bout, mad-a-bout lur-in' ev-'ry lad-a-bout, while leav-ing me moan-ing low, "Oh Fi-re-fly, __ why can't I latch on __ to you no-how? __ Oh, how I love ya but gee while you set the night on fire, fly, __ shine a lit-tle light on me!"

GET ON THE RIGHT THING

Words and Music by
McCARTNEY

All at once __ you get love on your mind __ And your world __ is as kind __ as a pen-ny.
All at once __ you get sound in your ears __ And your cloud __ dis-ap-pears __ in-to yel-low. Well, you know __
All at once __ we see things in our skies __ And we both __ re-a-lize __ it to-geth-er.

Oh, __ they were wrong. Get on the right thing. __
Well you knew it all __ a-long, __ you did the right thing, __ Be
Well you knew it all __ a-long, __ get on the right thing, __ Be
Yes, you knew it all __ a-long, __ get on the right thing, __ But be

lieve me, it's true ___ And it can hap-pen to you. ___
lieve me, it's so ___ Be - cause I hap-pen to know. ___
lieve me, it's so ___ Be - cause I hap-pen to know. ___

My lit - tle love, ___ it can't go wrong. (Get on the right thing, get on the right thing.)
My ti - ny love, ___ It can't go wrong. (Get on the right thing, get on the right thing.)

Now. (Get on the right thing.) Well, my lit - tle love, it can't go wrong. (Get on the right thing, get on the right thing,
Now. (Get on the right thing.) My ti - ny love,

get on the right thing.) Do. Get on the right thing, you.

(Get on the right thing, get on the right thing, Get on the right thing, get on the right thing.)

GO, MUSTANGS, GO!

By MILO SWEET

Go, ___ you Mus - tangs, through ___ that line! Driv - ing, pass - ing, score ___ this time! Show them ___ that

you're out to win. So, fight, fight, our Mus - tangs won't give in! Go, ___ you

Mus - tangs, keep ___ your stride! On ___ to vic - t'ry we ___ will ride! You're

"tops" ___ and up there to stay. This is our vic - t'ry day! ___

GARY, INDIANA
(From "The Music Man")

By MEREDITH WILLSON

GIVE A LITTLE WHISTLE
(From the Musical Production "Wildcat")

Lyric by CAROLYN LEIGH
Music by CY COLEMAN

GOIN' DOWN

Words and Music by
GREGORY GUIDRY & DAVID MARTIN

GET ON THE RIGHT TRACK, BABY

Words and Music by
TITUS TURNER

GETTING CLOSER

Words and Music by
McCARTNEY

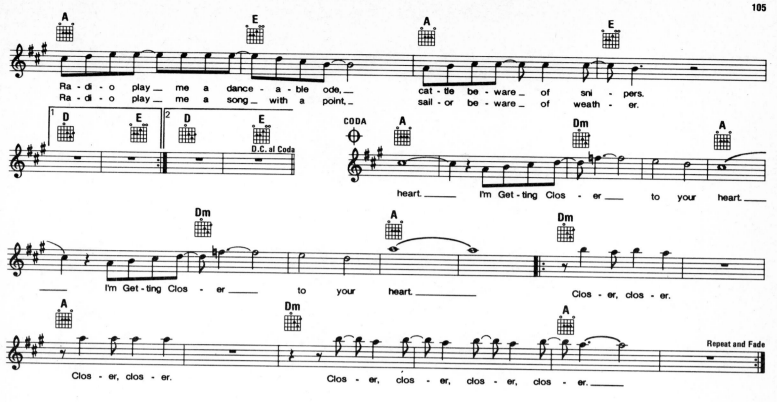

Ra - di - o play __ me a dance - a - ble ode, __ cat - tle be - ware __ of sni - pers.
Ra - di - o play __ me a song __ with a point, __ sail - or be - ware __ of weath - er.

CODA

heart. _____ I'm Get - ting Clos - er ____ to your heart. _____

I'm Get - ting Clos - er ____ to your heart. _____ Clos - er, clos - er.

Clos - er, clos - er. Clos - er, clos - er, clos - er, clos - er. _____ Repeat and Fade

THE GIFT!
(Recado Bossa Nova)

English Words by
PAUL FRANCIS WEBSTER
Original Words and Music by
DJALMA FERREIRA & LUIZ ANTONIO

Moderately, with a beat

No strings of pearls in a vel - vet glove, The gift I bring you is the gift of love.
gift of love is a pre - cious thing, A touch of mag - ic on a day in Spring.
kiss me sweet till our se - cret star il - lum - i - nates the way to Shan - gri - la!

To Coda

No ring of gold but a dream to en - fold when all the stars have flown __ and we're a - lone. __ The
The gold - en dream ev - 'ry dream - er pur -
What - ev - er fate may be - fall all I

sues, re - mem - ber dar - ling nev - er re - fuse the gift of love. _____ For love can be a mel -

- o - dy that ling - ers, __ Or slip like A - pril wine __ right thru your fing - ers. __

D.S. al Coda

CODA

So know is that the gift of love is the great - est gift of all. _____

GIRLS' SCHOOL

Words and Music by
McCARTNEY

GIRLFRIEND

Words and Music by
McCARTNEY

GO ON, BRUINS

By GORDON G. HOLMQUIST,
MILO SWEET and GWEN SWEET

GIVE IRELAND BACK TO THE IRISH

Words and Music by
McCARTNEY

GYPSYS, TRAMPS AND THIEVES

Words and Music by
ROBERT STONE

A GOOD MAN IS HARD TO FIND

By EDDIE GREEN

GO NORTHWESTERN GO
(Go U Northwestern)

By THEO. C. VAN ETTEN

THE GOOD TIMES ARE COMIN'
(From the Motion Picture "Monte Walsh")

Music by JOHN BARRY
Lyric by HAL DAVID

GOODNIGHT, MY SOMEONE
(From "The Music Man")

By MEREDITH WILLSON

GREASED LIGHTNIN'
(From "Grease")

Lyric and Music by
WARREN CASEY and JIM JACOBS

GOODNIGHT TONIGHT

By McCARTNEY

GRAZING IN THE GRASS

Words by HARRY ELSTON
Music by PHILEMON HOU

THE GRIDIRON KING

By RICHMOND K. FLETCHER '08

GUYS AND DOLLS
(From "Guys And Dolls")

By FRANK LOESSER

GREEN-EYED LADY

Words and Music by
JERRY CORBETTA, J.C. PHILLIPS
and DAVID RIORDAN

HE

Words by RICHARD MULLAN
Music by JACK RICHARDS

GRANDPA'S SPELLS

By FERD (JELLY ROLL) MORTON

HAIL, ALMA MATER

Words and Music by
PAUL YODER

HALF-BREED

Lyrics by MARY DEAN
Music by AL CAPPS

HAIL! MINNESOTA
(The Official State Song of Minnesota)

First Verse by TRUMAN E. RICKARD,
Second Verse by ARTHUR E. UPSON
Music by TRUMAN E. RICKARD

HELEN WHEELS

Words and Music by
McCARTNEY

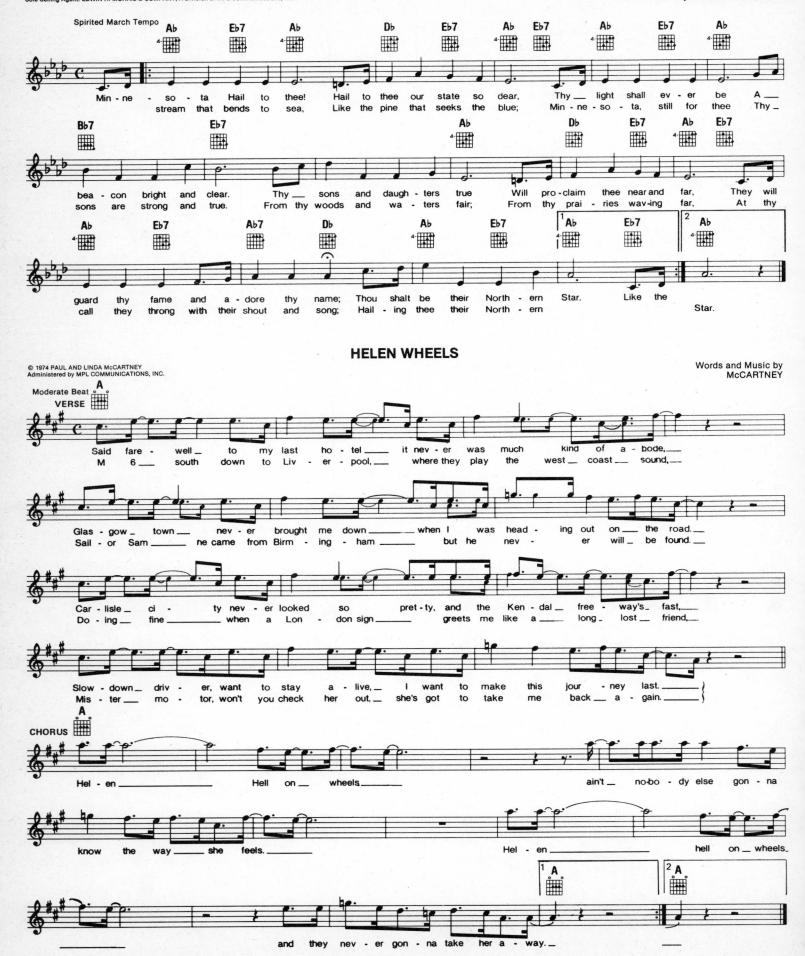

HAIL PURDUE

Words by J. MORRISON
Music by E.J. WOTAWA

HEARTBREAKER

Words and Music by
CAROLE BAYER SAGER & DAVID WOLFERT

HEART
(From "Damn Yankees")

Words and Music by
RICHARD ADLER and JERRY ROSS

HARD HEARTED HANNAH
(The Vamp Of Savannah)

Words and Music by
JACK YELLEN, MILTON AGER,
BOB BIGELOW and CHAS. BATES

Leath - er is tough, but Han - nah's heart is tough - er; She's a gal __ who loves to see men suf - fer! To
Talk of your cold, re - frig - er - at - ing Mam - mas, Broth - er, she's the Po - lar bear's pa - jam - as! To

tease 'em and thrill 'em, To tor - ture and kill 'em, Is her de - light, they say, __ I saw her at the sea - shore with a
tease 'em and thrill 'em, To tor - ture and kill 'em, Is her de - light, they say, __ An ev - 'ning spent with Han - nah sit - ting

great big pan; __ There was Han - nah pour - ing wa - ter on a drown - ing man, __ She's Hard Heart - ed Han - nah, The
on your knees, Is like trav - 'ling thru A - las - ka in your B. V. D's; __ She's Hard Heart - ed Han - nah, The

Vamp of Sa - van - nah G.   A.
Vamp of Sa - van - nah G.

They call her

A. _____

HELLO, DOLLY!
(From the Musical Production "Hello, Dolly!")

Music and Lyric by
JERRY HERMAN

Medium Strut tempo

Hel - lo, Dol - ly, well, Hel - lo, Dol - ly, It's so nice to have you back where you be - long. You're look - ing

swell, Dol - ly, we can tell, Dol - ly, You're still glow - in', you're still crow - in', you're still go - in' strong. We feel the

room sway - in', for the band's play - in' one of your old fa - v'rite songs from 'way back when. So

take her wrap, fel - las, Find her an emp - ty lap, fel las, Dol - ly 'll nev - er go a - way a - gain!
gol - ly gee, fel - las, Find her a va - cant knee, fel - las, Dol - ly 'll nev - er go a - way a - gain! Hel -

go a - way, Dol - ly 'll nev - er go a - way, Dol - ly 'll nev - er go a - way a - gain! _____

HEART OF THE COUNTRY

Words and Music by
McCARTNEY

HELLO TWELVE, HELLO THIRTEEN, HELLO LOVE
(From the Musical Production "A Chorus Line")

Music by MARVIN HAMLISCH
Lyric by EDWARD KLEBAN

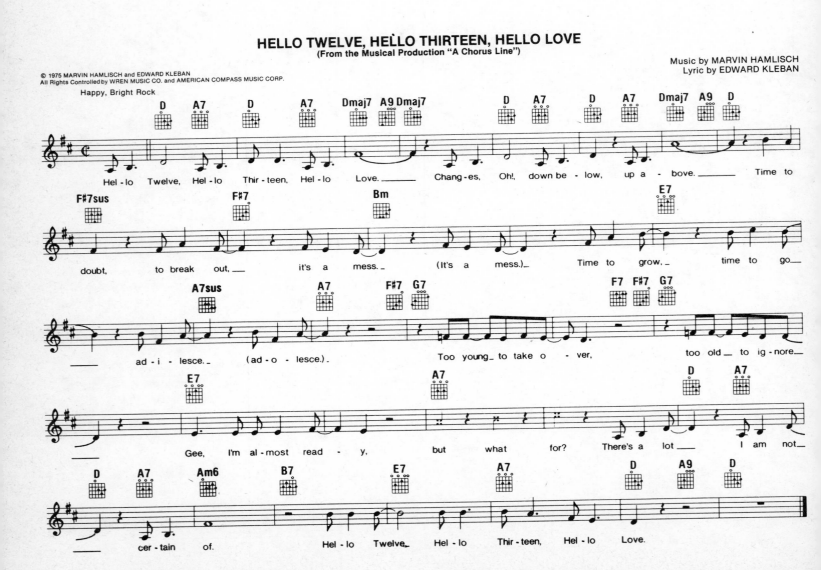

Heartbeat

Moderately

Words and Music by
BOB MONTGOMERY and NORMAN PETTY

Heart - beat, _____ why do you miss when_ my ba - by kiss - es me?
Heart - beat, _____ why do you skip when_ my ba - by's lips _ meet mine?

Heart - beat, _____
Heart - beat, _____

_____ why does a love kiss _ stay in my mem - o - ry?
_____ why do you flip, then give me a skip - beat sign?

Rid - dle - dee - pat, _ I know that new _ love thrills me. _
Rid - dle - dee - pat, _ and sing to me _ love's sto - ry. _

I know that true _ love will be. _____
And bring to me _ love's glo - ry. _____

Heart - beat, _____ why do you
Heart - beat, _____ why do you

miss when my ba - by kiss - es me?
miss when my ba - by kiss - es me?

HELLO MARY LOU

Words and Music by
GENE PITNEY

Moderately

Verse

You passed me by one sun - ny day ____ Flashed those big brown eyes my way and oo I want - ed you for - ev - er
(1) saw your lips I heard your voice _ Be - lieve me I just had no choice, wild hors - es could - n't make me stay a -

more. _____ Now I'm not one that gets a - round,. I swear my feet stuck to the ground, And though I nev - er
way. _____ I thought a - bout a moon - lit night, _ My arms a - bout you good an' tight, That's all I had to

did meet you be - fore. _____ I said "Hel - lo Ma - ry Lou

see for me to say. _____

Chorus

Good - bye heart Sweet

Ma - ry Lou I'm so in love with you. _____ I knew Ma - ry Lou We'd nev - er

part so Hel - lo Ma - ry Lou Good - bye heart." I heart."

HERE TODAY

Words and Music by
McCARTNEY

HOOTENANNY SATURDAY NIGHT

Words by ALFRED UHRY
Music by RICHARD LEWINE

FAR ABOVE CAYUGA'S WATERS

By C. URGUHART

FIVE FOOT TWO, EYES OF BLUE
(Has Anybody Seen My Girl?)

Words by JOE YOUNG & SAM LEWIS
Music by RAY HENDERSON

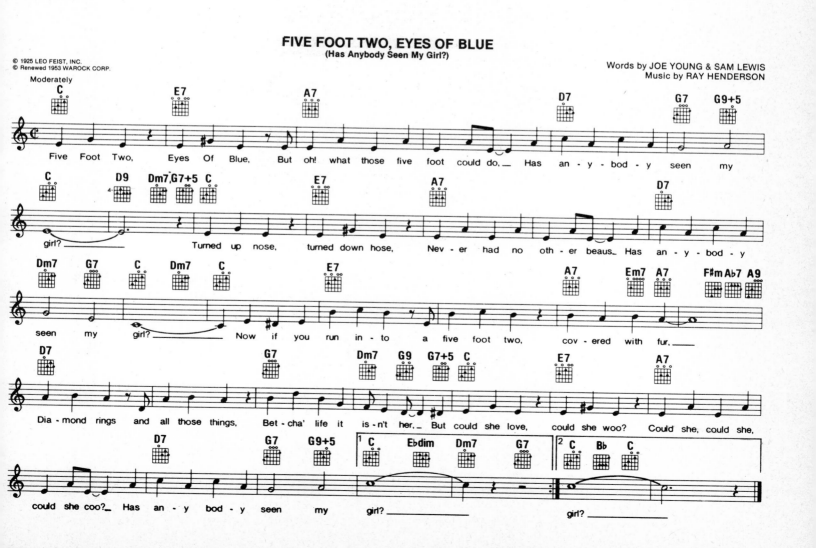

FAMOUS GROUPIES

Words and Music by
McCARTNEY

FIGHT ON

By MILO SWEET
and GLEN GRANT

Flamingo

Lyric by ED ANDERSON
Music by TED GROUYA

FOR EVERY MAN THERE'S A WOMAN
(From the Motion Picture "Casbah")

Lyric by LEO ROBIN
Music by HAROLD ARLEN

FUGUE FOR TINHORNS
(From "Guys And Dolls")

By FRANK LOESSER

FREEDOM
(From the Musical Production "Shenandoah")

Lyric by PETER UDELL
Music by GARY GELD

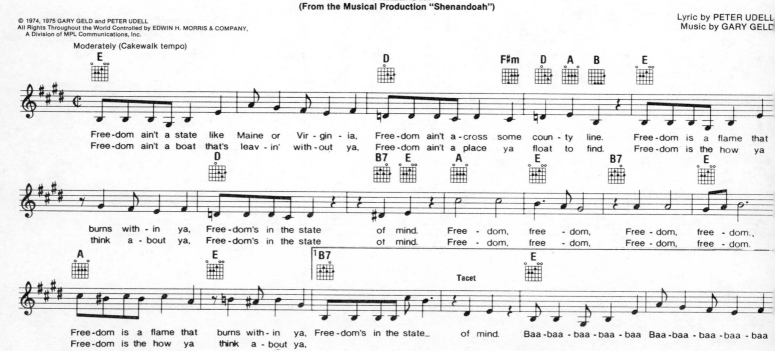

FROM THE LAND OF THE SKY-BLUE WATER

Lyric by NELLE RICHMOND EBERHART
Music by CHARLES WAKEFIELD CADMAN

FREDDY, MY LOVE
(From the Musical Production "Grease")

Lyric and Music by WARREN CASEY and JIM JACOBS

FALLEN ANGEL

Words and Music by WAYNE P. WALKER,
WEBB PIERCE & MARIJOHN WILKIN

Last night I saw an an-gel the one I once called mine The hand that wore my wed-ding band held a glass of
man-y times she told me she could-n't take much more So man-y times I laughed at her and walked right out the

wine I took her love for grant-ed I wronged her night and day I drove my an-gel from me and
door I was-n't wor-thy of her and now my an-gel's gone The de-vil took her from me and

now she's gone a-stray She's just a Fal-len An-gel but I don't blame her for it all She's just a
claimed her for his own

Fall-en An-gel and I'm the fool who made her fall So fall

FOUR BROTHERS

By JIMMIE GIUFFRE

FIREFLY

Lyric by CAROLYN LEIGH
Music by CY COLEMAN

GET ON THE RIGHT THING

Words and Music by
McCARTNEY

GO, MUSTANGS, GO!

By MILO SWEET

GARY, INDIANA
(From "The Music Man")

By MEREDITH WILLSON

GIVE A LITTLE WHISTLE
(From the Musical Production "Wildcat")

Lyric by CAROLYN LEIGH
Music by CY COLEMAN

GOIN' DOWN

Words and Music by
GREGORY GUIDRY & DAVID MARTIN

GET ON THE RIGHT TRACK, BABY

Words and Music by
TITUS TURNER

GETTING CLOSER

Words and Music by
McCARTNEY

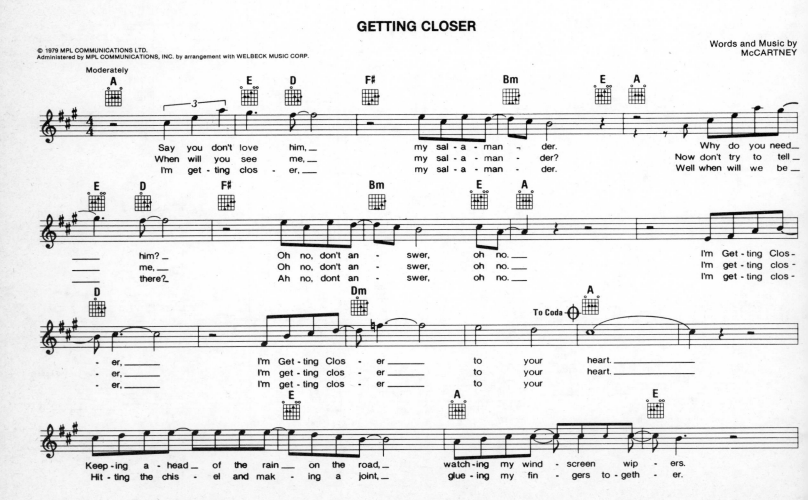

Radio play __ me a dance - a - ble ode, __ cat - tle be - ware __ of sni - pers.
Radio play __ me a song __ with a point, __ sail - or be - ware __ of weath - er.

D.C. al Coda

CODA

heart. _____ I'm Get - ting Clos - er __ to your heart. _____

I'm Get - ting Clos - er __ to your heart. _____ Clos - er, clos - er.

Repeat and Fade

Clos - er, clos - er. Clos - er, clos - er, clos - er, clos - er. _____

THE GIFT!
(Recado Bossa Nova)

English Words by
PAUL FRANCIS WEBSTER
Original Words and Music by
DJALMA FERREIRA & LUIZ ANTONIO

© 1959, 1963 RYTVOC, INC.

Moderately, with a beat

No strings of pearls in a vel - vet glove, The gift I bring you is the gift of love.
gift of love is a pre - cious thing, A touch of mag - ic on a day in Spring.
kiss me sweet till our se - cret star il - lum - i - nates the way to Shan - gri - la!

To Coda

No ring of gold but a dream to en - fold when all the stars have flown __ and we're a - lone. __ The
The gold - en dream ev - 'ry dream - er pur -
What - ev - er fate may be - fall all I

sues, re - mem - ber dar - ling nev - er re - fuse the gift of love. _____ For love can be a mel -

- o - dy that ling - ers, __ Or slip like A - pril wine __ right thru your fing - ers. __

D.S. al Coda

CODA

So know is that the gift of love is the great - est gift of all. _____

GIRLS' SCHOOL

Words and Music by
McCARTNEY

Sleep-y head kid sis-ter ly-ing on the floor.___ Eight-een years and young-

-er, boy___ and she knows what she's wait-ing for. ___ Yu-ki's a cool school mis-tress

She's an o-ri-en-tal prin-cess ___ She shows films in the class-room, boy___ they put the

pa-per on the win-dow ___ Ah, ___ what can the Sis-ters do? ___ Ah ___

Girls' School.

Well now Head nurse is Sis-ter Sca-la, now she's a Span-ish doll.
Rox-anne's the wom-an train-er, she puts the kids to bed.___

She runs a full bod-y out call mas-sage par-lor from the teach-er's hall
She gives them pills in a pa-per cup and she knocks them on the head.___

Repeat and Fade

D.S. al Coda

CODA

Ooh, ooh ___

GIRLFRIEND

Words and Music by
McCARTNEY

Girl-friend_ I'm gon-na tell your boy-friend_ yeah, ___ tell him _ ex-act-ly what you're
Girl-friend,_ I'm gon-na show your boy-friend,_ yeah, ___ show him _ the let-ters I've been

do-ing,_ yeah,_ tell him what you do to me ___ late at night ___ when the wind is free,_
sav-ing,_ yeah,_ show him how you feel in-side. _____ Then our love

GO ON, BRUINS

By GORDON G. HOLMQUIST,
MILO SWEET and GWEN SWEET

GIVE IRELAND BACK TO THE IRISH

Words and Music by
McCARTNEY

GYPSYS, TRAMPS AND THIEVES

Words and Music by
ROBERT STONE

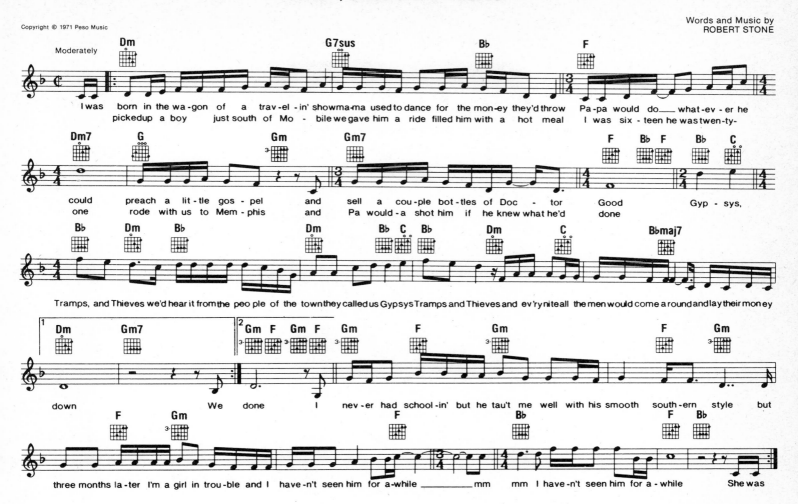

A GOOD MAN IS HARD TO FIND

By EDDIE GREEN

GO NORTHWESTERN GO
(Go U Northwestern)

By THEO. C. VAN ETTEN

THE GOOD TIMES ARE COMIN'
(From the Motion Picture "Monte Walsh")

Music by JOHN BARRY
Lyric by HAL DAVID

GOODNIGHT, MY SOMEONE
(From "The Music Man")

By MEREDITH WILLSON

GREASED LIGHTNIN'
(From "Grease")

Lyric and Music by
WARREN CASEY and JIM JACOBS

GOODNIGHT TONIGHT

By McCARTNEY

GRAZING IN THE GRASS

Words by HARRY ELSTON
Music by PHILEMON HOU

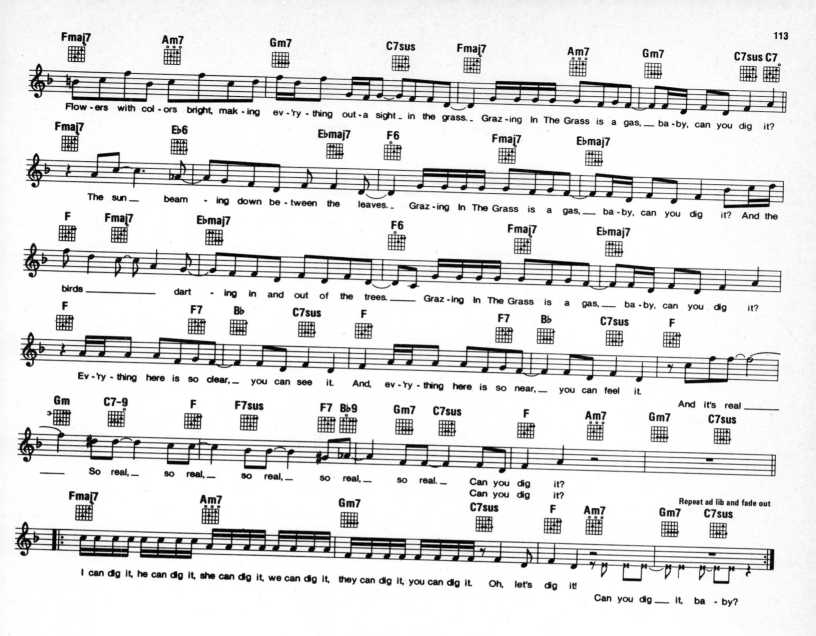

THE GRIDIRON KING

By RICHMOND K. FLETCHER '08

GUYS AND DOLLS
(From "Guys And Dolls")

By FRANK LOESSER

GREEN-EYED LADY

Words and Music by
JERRY CORBETTA, J.C. PHILLIPS
and DAVID RIORDAN

la - dy, _____ dressed in love _____ she lives _ for life _ to be. _____

Green - Eyed La - dy feels _ life I nev - er see set - ting sons _____ and lone - ly lov - ers free.

Fine   Tacet

D.C. al Fine

HE

Words by RICHARD MULLAN
Music by JACK RICHARDS

Moderately Slow

He   can turn the tides   and calm the an - gry sea.   He   a - lone de - cides   who writes a sym - pho -
He   can grant a wish   or make a dream   come true.   He   can paint the clouds   and turn the gray   to

ny.   He   lights ev - 'ry star   that makes our dark - ness bright.   He   keeps watch all through   each long and
blue.   He   a - lone knows where   to find the rain - bow's end.   He   a - lone can see   what lies be -

lone - ly night.   He   still finds the time   to hear a child's   first prayer.   Saint   or sin - ner
yond   the bend.   He   can touch a tree   and turn the leaves   to gold.   He   knows ev - 'ry

call   and al - ways find   Him there.   } Though   it makes Him sad   to see the way   we live, He'll al - ways
lie   that you and I   have told. {

say,   "I   for - give." _____

give, _____   I   for - give."

GRANDPA'S SPELLS

By FERD (JELLY ROLL) MORTON

HAIL, ALMA MATER

Words and Music by
PAUL YODER

HALF-BREED

Lyrics by MARY DEAN
Music by AL CAPPS

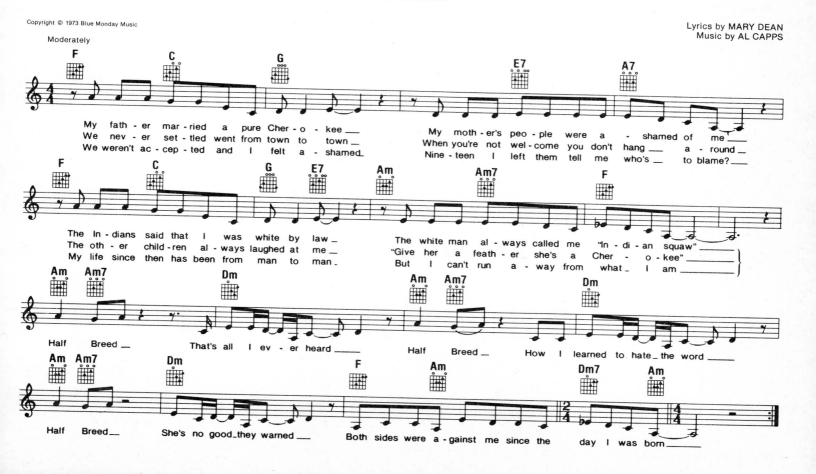

HAIL! MINNESOTA
(The Official State Song of Minnesota)

First Verse by TRUMAN E. RICKARD,
Second Verse by ARTHUR E. UPSON
Music by TRUMAN E. RICKARD

HELEN WHEELS

Words and Music by
McCARTNEY

HAIL PURDUE

Words by J. Morrison
Music by E.J. WOTAWA

HEARTBREAKER

Words and Music by
CAROLE BAYER SAGER & DAVID WOLFERT

HEART
(From "Damn Yankees")

Words and Music by
RICHARD ADLER and JERRY ROSS

© 1955 FRANK MUSIC CORP.

HARD HEARTED HANNAH
(The Vamp Of Savannah)

Words and Music by
JACK YELLEN, MILTON AGER,
BOB BIGELOW and CHAS. BATES

© 1924, 1955 ADVANCED MUSIC CORPORATION
© Renewed 1952 EDWIN H. MORRIS & COMPANY, A Division of MPL Communications, Inc.

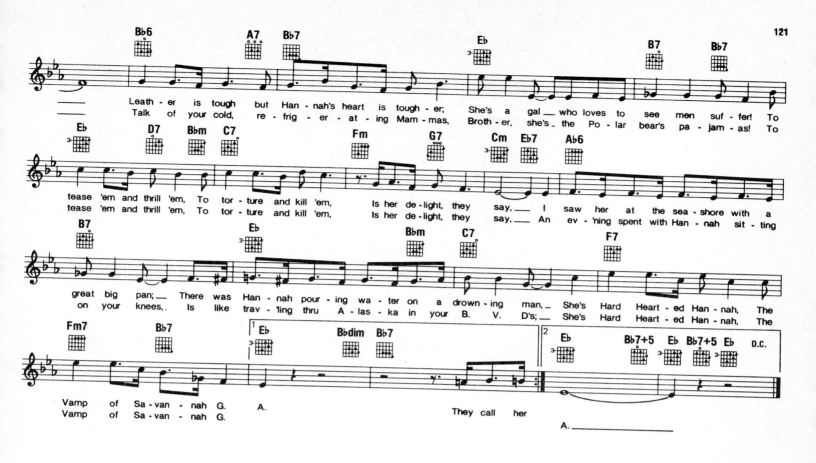

Leath - er is tough but Han - nah's heart is tough - er; She's a gal __ who loves to see men suf - fer! To
Talk of your cold, re - frig - er - at - ing Mam - mas, Broth - er, she's the Po - lar bear's pa - jam - as! To

tease 'em and thrill 'em, To tor - ture and kill 'em, Is her de - light, they say, __ I saw her at the sea - shore with a
tease 'em and thrill 'em, To tor - ture and kill 'em, Is her de - light, they say, __ An ev - 'ning spent with Han - nah sit - ting

great big pan; There was Han - nah pour - ing wa - ter on a drown - ing man, __ She's Hard Heart - ed Han - nah, The
on your knees,. Is like trav - 'ling thru A - las - ka in your B. V. D's; __ She's Hard Heart - ed Han - nah, The

Vamp of Sa - van - nah G. A.
Vamp of Sa - van - nah G.

They call her

A. _____

HELLO, DOLLY!
(From the Musical Production "Hello, Dolly!")

Music and Lyric by
JERRY HERMAN

Medium Strut tempo

Hel - lo, Dol - ly, well, Hel - lo, Dol - ly, It's so nice to have you back where you be - long. You're look - ing

swell, Dol - ly, we can tell, Dol - ly, You're still glow - in', you're still crow - in', you're still go - in' strong. We feel the

room sway - in', for the band's play - in' one of your old fa - v'rite songs from 'way back when. So

take her wrap, fel - las, Find her an emp - ty lap, fel las, Dol - ly 'll nev - er go a - way a - gain! Hel -
gol - ly gee, fel - las, Find her a va - cant knee, fel - las,

go a - way, Dol - ly 'll nev - er go a - way, Dol - ly 'll nev - er go a - way a - gain! _____

HEART OF THE COUNTRY

Words and Music by
McCARTNEY

HELLO TWELVE, HELLO THIRTEEN, HELLO LOVE

(From the Musical Production "A Chorus Line")

Music by MARVIN HAMLISCH
Lyric by EDWARD KLEBAN

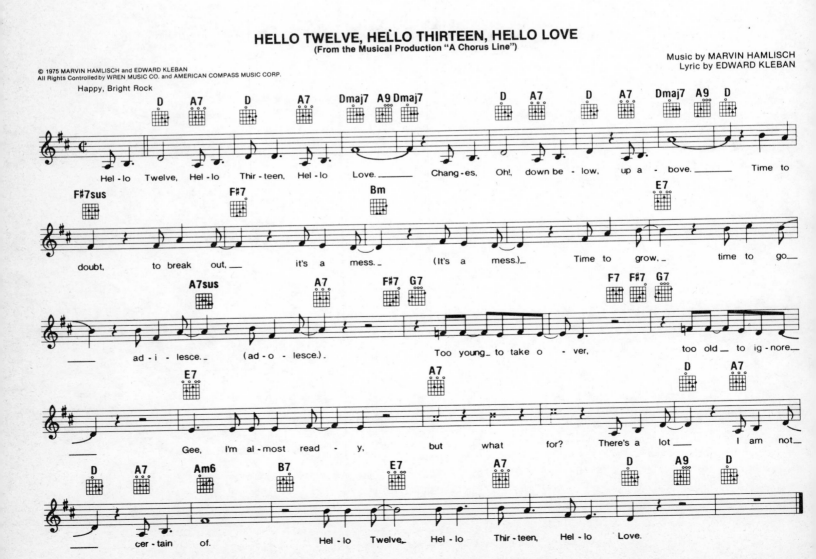

HEARTBEAT

Moderately

Words and Music by
BOB MONTGOMERY and NORMAN PETTY

Heart - beat, _____ why do you miss when_ my ba - by kiss - es me?
Heart - beat, _____ why do you skip when_ my ba - by's lips _ meet mine?

Heart - beat, _____
Heart - beat, _____

_____ why does a love kiss_ stay in my mem - o - ry?
_____ why do you flip, then_ give me a skip - beat sign?

Rid - dle - dee - pat, _ I know that new _ love thrills me,
Rid - dle - dee - pat, _ and sing to me _ love's sto - ry. _

I know that true _ love will be. _____
And bring to me _ love's glo - ry. _____

Heart - beat, _____ why do you
Heart - beat, _____ why do you

miss when my ba - by kiss - es me?
miss when my ba - by kiss - es me?

HELLO MARY LOU

Words and Music by
GENE PITNEY

Moderately
Verse

You passed me by one sun - ny day ___ Flashed those big brown eyes my way and oo I want - ed you for - ev - er
(I) saw your lips I heard your voice _ Be - lieve me I just had no choice, wild hors - es could - n't make me stay a -

more. _____ Now I'm not one that gets a - round,. I swear my feet stuck to the ground, And though I nev - er
way. _____ I thought a - bout a moon - lit night,_ My arms a - bout you good an' tight, That's all I had to

did meet you be - fore. _____ I said "Hel - lo Ma - ry Lou Good - bye heart Sweet
see for me to say. _____

Chorus

Ma - ry Lou I'm so in love with you. _____ I knew Ma - ry Lou We'd nev - er

part so Hel - lo Ma - ry Lou Good - bye heart." _____ I heart." _____

HERE TODAY

Words and Music by
McCARTNEY

And if I said I real-ly knew__ you well,__ what would your ans-wer be,__ if you were here__ to-day,__
And if I say I real-ly loved__ you and__ was glad you came a-long,__ then you were here__ to-day,__

ooh,_____ here to-day. Well know-ing you,__ you'd probab-ly laugh__ and say that we were worlds__ a-part,__
ooh,_____ here to-day.

if you were here__ to-day,__ ooh _____ here to-day. But as for me,__ I still re-mem-ber how it was__

____ be-fore, and I am hold-ing back the tears no more,__ ooh ooh ooh,__ I love_ you,

ooh. _____ What a-bout the time we met,__ well I sup-pose that you could say that we were play-ing hard__ to get.

Did-n't un-der-stand a thing,__ but we could al-ways sing.__ What a-bout the night we cried,__ be-cause there

was-n't an-y rea-son left to keep it all __ in-side. Nev-er un-der-stood a word,__ but you were

al-ways there _ with a smile. ____ ____ for you were in my song, _ ooh,_____ here to-day.

(D.C. (a tempo))

CODA

HOOTENANNY SATURDAY NIGHT

Words by ALFRED UHRY
Music by RICHARD LEWINE

Moderately

We'll have a Hoot-'nan-ny, Hoot-'nan-ny Sat-ur-day Night.__ We'll raise the roof and the raft-ers with song.____
Hoot-'nan-ny, Hoot-'nan-ny Sat-ur-day Night.__ And if you think we'll be row-dy, you're

Tacet

Yell out your fav-'rite, We'll sing it loud and strong. Come and bring your la-dy love a-long._____ We'll throw a right!

____ We'll hoot and hol-ler and raise al-might-y cain Ev-'ry Sat-ur-day night.__

I'VE GOTTA CROW
(From "Peter Pan")

Lyric by CAROLYN LEIGH
Music by MARK CHARLAP

IF I DIDN'T CARE

Words and Music by JACK LAWRENCE

IF HE WALKED INTO MY LIFE

(From the Musical Production "Mame")

Music and Lyric by JERRY HERMAN

IF I HAD A MILLION DOLLARS

Words and Music by PINKY HERMAN,
JOHNNY KAMANO & MAURIE HARTMANN

ILL WIND
(You're Blowin' Me No Good)

Lyric by TED KOEHLER
Music by HAROLD ARLEN

IF I WERE A BELL
(From "Guys And Dolls")

By FRANK LOESSER

THE INCH WORM
(From "Hans Christian Andersen")

By FRANK LOESSER

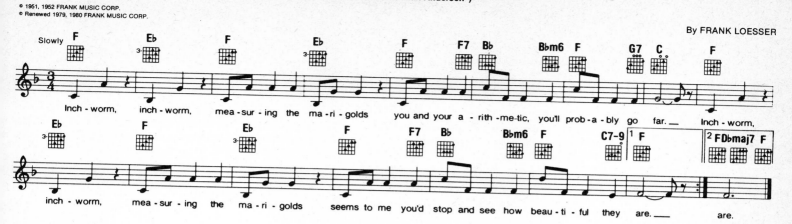

Inch - worm, inch - worm, mea - sur - ing the ma - ri - golds you and your a - rith - me - tic, you'll prob - a - bly go far. __ Inch - worm,

inch - worm, mea - sur - ing the ma - ri - golds seems to me you'd stop and see how beau - ti - ful they are. __ are.

IT NEVER RAINS IN SOUTHERN CALIFORNIA

Words and Music by
ALBERT HAMMOND & MIKE HAZLEWOOD

Got on board __ a west - bound. Sev - en For - ty Sev - en. __ Did - n't think __

__ be - fore __ de - cid - ing what __ to do. __ All that talk of op - por - tun -

- i - ties, T. V. breaks __ and mov - ies __ rang true, __ sure rang __ true. __

__ Seems It Nev - er Rains __ In South - ern __ Cal - i - for - nia. __ Seems I've of -

- ten heard __ that kind __ of talk __ be - fore. __ It nev - er rains in Cal - i - for -

- nia, __ But girl, don't they warn __ 'ya, __ It pours, __ man it pours. __

Out of work, I'm out a' my head, __ Out of self - re - spect, I'm out a' bread. __ I'm un - der -

loved, I'm un - der - fed, __ I wan - na go home. __ It Nev - er

IN THE STILL OF THE NIGHT
(I'll Remember)

Words and Music by FRED PARRIS

ILLINOIS LOYALTY
(We're Loyal To You, Illinois)

Words and Music by T.H. GUIL

IN A SHANTY IN OLD SHANTY TOWN

Words by JOE YOUNG
Music by LITTLE JACK LITTLE & JOHN SIRAS

IN A LITTLE SPANISH TOWN
('Twas On A Night Like This)

Words by SAM M. LEWIS & JOE YOU
Music by MABEL WAY

IN A LONG WHITE ROOM

Music by CLINT BALLARD
Words by MARTIN CHARM

share what must be shared   we'll hide what must be hid-den   and air what must be aired   we

are-n't that sure but   we are-n't that scared.   we will grow _____   In A Long White

Room _____   In A Long White Room _____   In A Long White Room. _____

IN THE MIDDLE OF AN ISLAND

Words and Music by NICK ACQUAVIVA & TED VARNICK

Moderately

In The Mid-dle Of An   Is - land   in the mid-dle of the o - cean   you and I be-neath the
Is - land   plen-ty time to do some kiss - in'   plen-ty time for lots of

moon - light   just the mon-keys and the palm   trees.   In The Mid-dle Of An
lov - in'   walk-ing bare-foot in the   sand.

Tho' there's no is - land at all,   just a pic-ture on my wall   my dar-ling, how I

wish we could be.   In The Mid-dle Of An Is - land   in the mid-dle of the o - cean

you and I for-ev-er, dar - ling   in our Par-a-dise for two.   We'll go two.   Fine

swim-ming ev-'ry day   and have fun _____   and we'll lay out on the beach   in the sun. _____   We'll eat

co-co-nuts and fish   and be free _____   to do the things that come nat-'ral-ly! _____   In The Mid-dle Of An

D.S. al Fine

INDISCREET
(From the Motion Picture "Indiscreet")

Words by SAMMY CAHN
Music by JAMES VAN HEUSEN

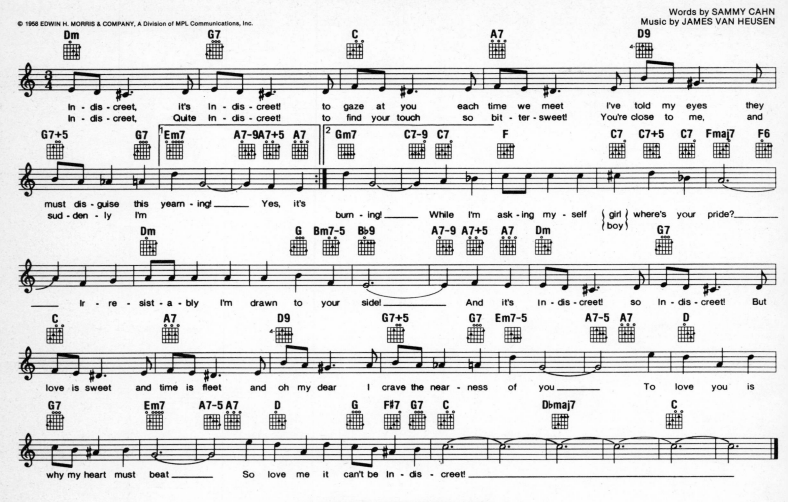

INCENSE AND PEPPERMINTS

Words and Music by JOHN CARTER & TIM GILBERT

IT ONLY TAKES A MOMENT
(From the Musical Production "Hello, Dolly!")

Music and Lyric by JERRY HERMAN

INDIANA, OUR INDIANA

Words and Music by
RUSSELL P. HARKER & K.L. KING

IT'S BEEN A LONG, LONG TIME

Lyric by SAMMY CAHN
Music by JULE STYNE

IT AMAZES ME

Lyric by CAROLYN LEIGH
Music by CY COLEMAN

Moderately, With Feeling

It A - maz - es Me ___ It sim - ply a - maz - es me ___ What she sees in me daz - zles me, da - zes me! ___
prais - es me ___ just know - ing I'd try for her ___ When so man - y would if they could,

That I've learned to clip my wings and sof - ten my ways ___ These are or - di - nar - y

things un - worth - y of praise ___ Yet she

die for her! ___ I'm the one who's world - ly

wise, and no - thing much faz - es me ___ But, to see me in her eyes it just a - maz - es me! ___

IT'S BEGINNING TO LOOK LIKE CHRISTMAS

By MEREDITH WILLSON

Moderately

It's Be - gin - ning To Look A Lot Like Christ - mas, Ev - 'ry - where you go; ___ {Take a look in the five and ten,
There's a tree in the grand ho - tel,

glis - ten - ing once a - gain, with can - dy canes and sil - ver lanes a - glow. It's Be - gin - ning To Look A Lot Like Christ - mas, toys in ev - 'ry
one in the park, as well, the stur - dy kind that does - n't mind the snow.

store ___ But the pret - ti - est sight to see is the hol - ly that will be, on your own front door ___ A pair of
start ___ And the thing that will make them ring is the ca - rol that you sing right with - in your heart ___

hop - a - long boots and a pis - tol that shoots is the wish of Bar - ney and Ben;
Dolls that will talk and will go for a walk is the

hope of Jan - ice and Jen; And mom and dad can hard - ly wait for school to start a - gain. It's Be -

I SAW THE LIGHT

Words and Music by
HANK WILLIAMS

IVORY TOWER

Words and Music by JACK FULTON & LOIS STEELE

IT'S A BIG WIDE WONDERFUL WORLD

Lyric and Music by
JOHN ROX

IT'S SO EASY

Words and Music by
BUDDY HOLLY and NORMAN PETTY

IT'S HARD TO BE HUMBLE

Words and Music by MAC DAVIS

IT'S THE HARD-KNOCK LIFE
(From the Musical Production "Annie")

Lyric by MARTIN CHARNIN
Music by CHARLES STROUSE

IOWA CORN SONG

Lyric by R.W. LOCKARD & GEORGE HAMILTON
Music by EDWARD RILEY & GEORGE BOTSFORD

IT'S SO NICE TO HAVE A MAN AROUND THE HOUSE

Lyric by JACK ELLIOTT
Music by HAROLD SPINA

IT'S TODAY

(From the Musical Production "Mame")

Music and Lyric by JERRY HERMAN

IVY
(From the Motion Picture "IVY")

Words and Music by
HOAGY CARMICHAEL

JESSE

Words and Music by
JANIS IAN

176

JET

Words and Music by
McCARTNEY

JOEY'S THEME
(From the Motion Picture "Little Fugitive")

Music by
EDDY MANSON

JOHN, JOHN

Words by EARL SHUMAN
Music by SHERMAN EDWARDS

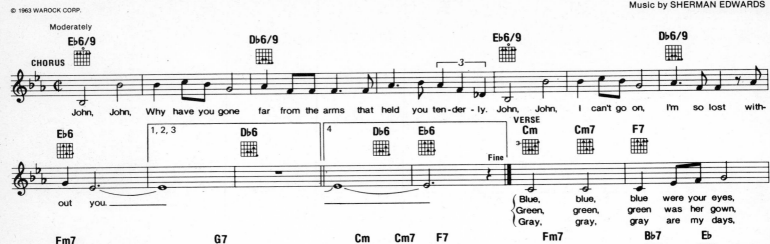

JOHNSON RAG

Lyric by JACK LAWRENCE
Music by GUY HALL and HENRY KLEINKAUF

JUNIOR'S FARM

Words and Music by
McCARTNEY

Moderately, with a steady beat

JOEY, JOEY, JOEY
(From "The Most Happy Fella")

By FRANK LOESSER

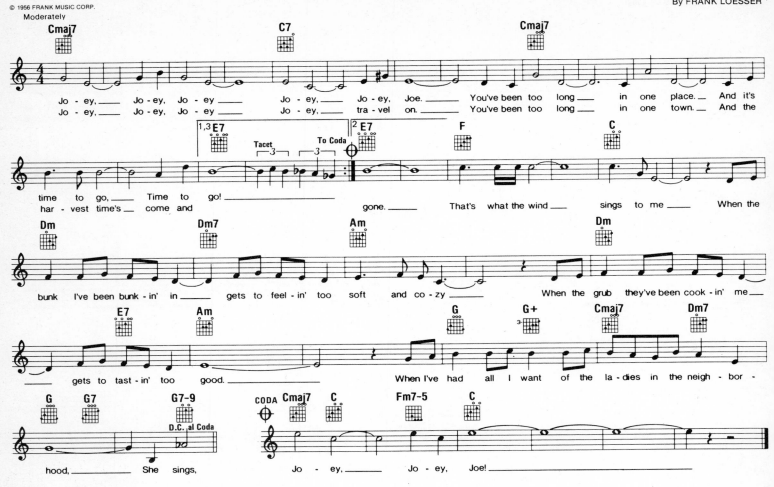

JUST GO TO THE MOVIES
(From "A Day In Hollywood")

Music and Lyric by
JERRY HERMAN

KIDS!
(From the Musical Production "Bye Bye Birdie")

Words by LEE ADAMS
Music by CHARLES STROUSE

Charleston tempo

JUST ANOTHER POLKA

Words and Music by
FRANK LOESSER & MILTON DeLUGG

JAMBALAYA
(On The Bayou)

Words and Music by
HANK WILLIAMS

Moderately

Good-bye, Joe, me got-ta go, me oh my oh ___ Me got-ta go pole the pi-rogue down the bay-ou ___ My Y-vonne, the sweet-est one, me oh my oh ___ Son of a gun, we'll have big fun on the bay-ou ___

daux, Fon-tain-eaux, the place is buzz-in' ___ Kin-folk come to see Y-vonne ___ by the doz-en ___ Dress in style and go hog wild, me oh my oh ___ Son of a gun, we'll have big fun on the bay-ou ___

Jam-ba-la-ya and a craw-fish pie and fil-let gum-bo ___ 'Cause to-night I'm gon-na see my ma cher a-mi-o ___ Pick gui-tar, fill fruit jar and be gay-o ___ Son of a gun, we'll have big fun on the bay-ou ___ thi-bo-bay-ou ___

KAW-LIGA

Words by FRED ROSE
Music by HANK WILLIAMS

Moderately

VERSE

Kaw-Li-ga was a wood-ed In-di-an stand-ing by ___ the door ___ He fell in love with an In-di-an maid-en o-ver in the an-tique store. Kaw-Li-ga ___ Just stood there and nev-er let it show ___ So she could nev-er an-swer "yes" or "no" ___ He

al-ways wore his Sun-day feath-ers and held a tom-a-hawk. The maid-en wore her ___ beads. and braids and hoped. some___day he'd talk. Kaw-Li-ga ___ Too stub-born to ev-er show a sign ___ Be-cause his heart was made of knot-ty pine ___

CHORUS

Poor ol' Kaw-Li-ga, he nev-er got a kiss Poor ol' Kaw-Li-ga, he don't know what he missed Is it an-y won-der that his face is red Kaw-Li-ga, that poor ol' wood-en head ___ Kaw-head. ___

Verse 2 (Kaw)-liga was a lonely Indian, never went nowhere
His heart was set on the Indian maiden with the coal black hair.
Kaw-liga just stood there and never let it show so she could never
answer "yes" or "no"

And then one day a wealthly customer bought the Indian maid and took
her, oh, so far away but ol' Kaw-liga stayed.
Kaw-liga just stands there as lonely as can be and wishes he was still
an old pine.

KEEPIN' OUT OF MISCHIEF NOW

Words by ANDY RAZAF
Music by THOMAS "FATS" WALLER

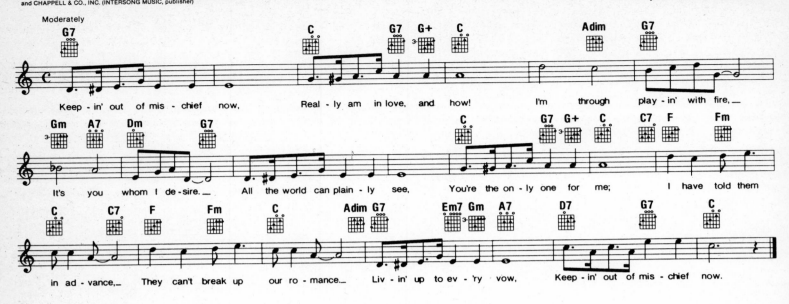

THE JOINT IS JUMPIN'

Words by ANDY RAZAF & J.C. JOHNSON
Music by THOMAS "FATS" WALLER

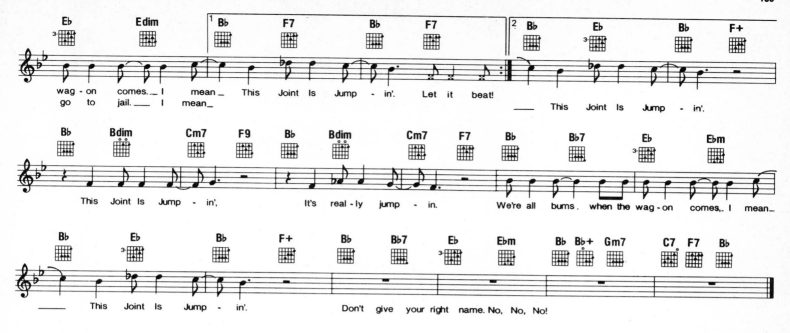

wag - on comes. __ I mean __ This Joint Is Jump - in'. Let it beat!
go to jail. __ I mean __

__ This Joint Is Jump - in'.

This Joint Is Jump - in', It's real - ly jump - in. We're all bums. when the wag - on comes, __ I mean __

__ This Joint Is Jump - in'. Don't give your right name. No, No, No!

KNOCK THREE TIMES

Words and Music by
IRWIN LEVINE & L. RUSSELL BROWN

Hey, girl, what - cha do - in' down there? Danc - in' a - lone ev - 'ry night while I live right a - bove __ you. __
you look out your win - dow to - night, Pull in the string with the note that's at - tached to my heart. __

__ I can hear your mu - sic play - in', __ I can feel your bod - y sway - in', __
Read how man - y times I saw __ you, __ How in my si - lence I a - dore __ you, And

One floor be - low me, you don't e - ven know me, I love __ you. Oh, my dar - lin',
on - ly in my dreams did that wall be - tween us come a - part. __

Knock Three Times on the ceil - ing if you want __ me; __ Twice on the pipe if the an - swer is

no. __ Oh, my sweet - ness, (Knock) means you'll meet me in the hall - way; __

Twice on the pipe means you ain't gon - na show. __ If Oh, my dar - lin',

D.S. and Fade

KEEP ON SINGING

Words and Music by
DANNY JANSSEN & BOBBY HART

KING PORTER STOMP

Music and Lyric by
FERDINAND "JELLY ROLL" MORTON,
SID ROBIN & SONNY BURKE

LOVE'S THEME

By BARRY WHITE

LET 'EM IN

Words and Music by
McCARTNEY

LAUGH! CLOWN! LAUGH!

Words by SAM M. LEWIS & JOE YOUNG
Music by TED FIORITO

LETTING GO

Words and Music by
McCARTNEY

LEAVE IT

© 1974 PAUL AND LINDA McCARTNEY
Administered by MPL COMMUNICATIONS, INC.

Words and Music by
McCARTNEY

THE LONG BLACK VEIL

Copyright © 1959 by CEDARWOOD PUBLISHING CO., INC., Nashville, TN

Words and Music by
MARIJOHN WILKIN & DANNY DILL

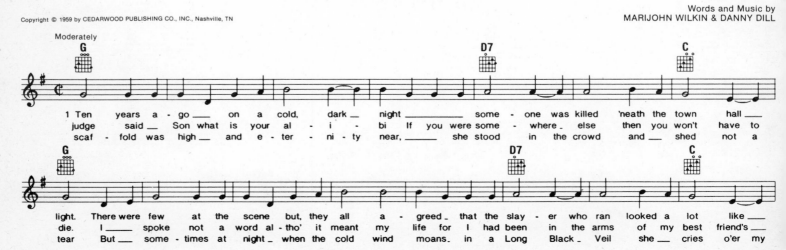

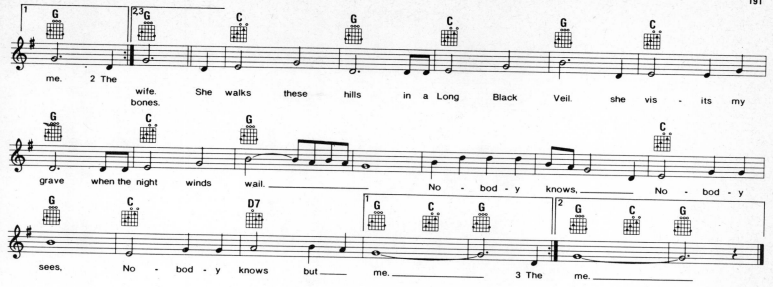

G | **G** | **C** | **G** | **C** | **G** | **C**

me. 2 The wife. She walks these hills in a Long Black Veil. she vis - its my

G | **C** | **G** | **C**

grave when the night winds wail. _____ No - bod - y knows, _____ No - bod - y

G | **C** | **D7** | **G** **C** **G** | **G** **C** **G**

sees, No - bod - y knows but _____ me. 3 The me.

LINDA

Words and Music by
JACK LAWRENCE

Slowly **G** | **G#dim** | **Am7** **D7**

When I go to sleep_ I nev - er count sheep,_ I count all the charms_ a - bout Lin - da._ And late - ly it seems_ in

D9 | **G** | **C** | **G**

all of my dreams_ I walk with my arms_ a - bout Lin - da._ But what good does_ it do me, _____ For

D7 **G** | **B7** | **Em** | **A7** | **Am7** **D7**

Lin - da does - n't know I ex - ist? _____ Can't help feel - ing gloom - y, _____ Think of all the lov - in' I've missed. _____ We

G | **G#dim** | **Am7** **D7**

pass on the street,_ my heart skips a beat,_ I say to my - self _____ "Hel - lo, Lin - da." _____ If on - ly she'd smile_ I'd

D9 | **G** | **C** | **G**

stop her a while _____ And then I would get_ to know Lin - da. _____ But mir - a - cles_ still hap - pen And

Dm **E7** | **Am7** | **F#dim** **G** **Am7** | **Cm** **G**

when my luck - y star be - gins to shine, _____ With one luck - y break_ I'll make Lin - da mine. _____

LUCK BE A LADY
(From "Guys And Dolls")

By FRANK LOESSER

THE LION IN WINTER
(From the Motion Picture "The Lion In Winter")

Music by JOHN BARRY

LIDA ROSE
(From "The Music Man")

By MEREDITH WILLSON

LITTLE HANDS
From "I, Anastasia" (Based on themes of S. Rachmaninoff)

Music and Lyric by
ROBERT WRIGHT & GEORGE FORREST

LINGER AWHILE

Words by LARRY OWENS
Music by VINCENT ROSE

LIVE AND LET DIE

Words and Music by
McCARTNEY

196

LIKE A STRAW IN THE WIND

Lyric by TED KOEHLER
Music by HAROLD ARLEN

© 1962 ARKO MUSIC CORP.

A LITTLE BRAINS, A LITTLE TALENT
(From "Damn Yankees")

Words and Music by
RICHARD ADLER & JERRY ROSS

© 1955, 1957 FRANK MUSIC CORP.

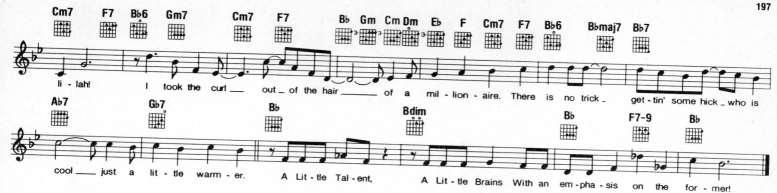

li - lah! I took the curl ___ out ___ of the hair ___ of a mil - lion - aire. There is no trick ___ get - tin' some hick ___ who is

cool ___ just a lit - tle warm - er. A Lit - tle Tal - ent, A Lit - tle Brains With an em - pha - sis on the for - mer!

LITTLE LAMB DRAGONFLY

Words and Music by
McCARTNEY

I have no an - swer for you, lit - tle lamb; ___ I can help you out, ___ But I can - not help you

in. Some - times you think that life is hard, And this is on - ly one of them.

My heart is break - ing for you, lit - tle lamb, ___ I can help you out, ___ But we may nev - er meet a - gain.

La ___ la la la ___ la la la La la la la ___ la la la la. La la ___ la la la

la la la ___ La la la la ___ la la ___ la.

Drag - on - fly, ___ fly by my win - dow. ___
Drag - on - fly, ___ don't keep me wait - ing. ___

You and I ___ still have a way ___ to go. ___ Don't know why ___ you hang a - round my door ___
When we try ___ we'll have a way ___ to go. ___ Drag - on - fly, ___ you've been a - way too long; ___

I don't live here an - y - more. } Since you've gone I nev - er know, ___ I go on, I miss ___ you so. ___
How did two rights make a wrong? }

In my heart ___ I feel the pain, ___ Keeps com - ing back ___ a - gain.

D.S. and Fade

LIVERY STABLE BLUES
(Barnyard Blues)

Lyric by MARVIN LEE
Music by RAY LOPEZ &
ALCIDE NUNEZ

LOLITA
(From the Musical Production "Lolita, My Love")

Lyric by ALAN JAY LERNER
Music by JOHN BARRY

A LITTLE STREET WHERE OLD FRIENDS MEET

By GUS KAHN
& HARRY WOODS

Moderate Waltz

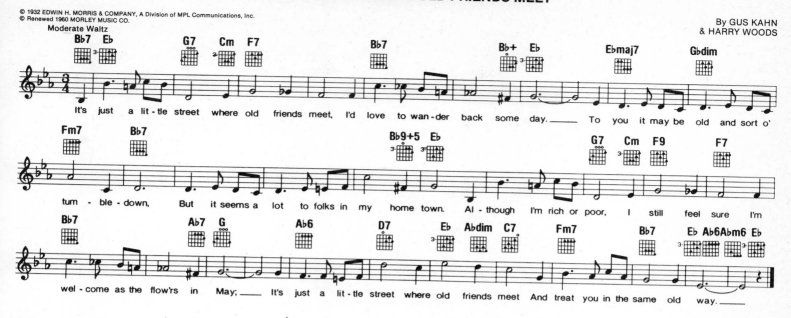

LONESOME TEARS

Words and Music by
BUDDY HOLLY

Moderately and Steadily

LEAVIN' ON YOUR MIND

Words and Music by
WAYNE P. WALKER & WEBB PIERCE

LONG LONESOME HIGHWAY

Words and Music by
JAMES HENDRICKS

LOVE ME DO

Words and Music by
JOHN LENNON & PAUL McCARTNEY

LOVE IS ONLY LOVE
(From the Motion Picture "Hello, Dolly!")

Music and Lyric by
JERRY HERMAN

A LOT OF LIVIN' TO DO
(From the Musical Production "Bye Bye Birdie")

Lyric by LEE ADAMS
Music by CHARLES STROUSE

With a steady, growing drive

Cmaj7 **C6** **Cmaj7** **C7** **F6** **Fmaj7**

There are {girls} {guys} just ripe for some kiss - in' And I mean to kiss me a few! Oh, those {girls} {guys}

G7 **C** **Dm7** **G7** **C** **Cmaj7**

don't know what they're miss - in', I've got A Lot Of Liv - in' To Do! {And there's wine} {siz - zlin' steaks} all read - y for

C6 **Cmaj7** **C7** **F6** **Fmaj7** **G7** **C**

tast - in' And there's Cad - il - lacs all shin - y and new! Got - ta move, 'cause time is a - wast - in',

Dm7 **G7** **C** **C7** **F6** **Fm7** **Eb**

There's such A Lot Of Liv - in' To Do! There's mu - sic to play, places to go! People to see!

Bb **G** **G7** **Cmaj7** **C6** **Cmaj7**

Ev - 'ry - thing for you and me! Life's a ball, if on - ly you know it! And it's all

C7 **F6** **Fmaj7** **G7** **C** **Dm7** **1. G7** **C**

just wait - in' for you! You're a - live, so come on and show it! There's such A Lot Of Liv - in' To Do!

G7 **2. G7** **Dm7** **G7** **Dm7** **G7-9** **C6**

There are Liv - in', Such A Lot Of Liv - in' What A Lot Of Liv - in' To Do!

LONDON TOWN

Words and Music by
McCARTNEY

Moderately

E **F#m7**

Walk - ing down the side - walk on a pur - ple af - ter - noon, I was ac - cost - ed by a bark - er
Crawl - ing down the pave - ment on a Sun - day af - ter - noon, I was ar - rest - ed by a roz - zer

B11 **E** **D** **A** **E** **B7**

play - ing a sim - ple tune up - on his flute.
wear - ing a pink bal - loon a - bout his foot.} Toot toot toot toot. Sil - ver rain was fall - ing down, up - on

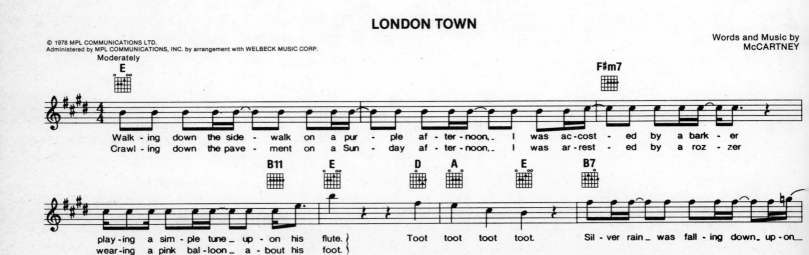

LOVE'S MADE A FOOL OF YOU

Words and Music by
BUDDY HOLLY & BOB MONTGOMERY

LET'S GO TO THE MOVIES
(From The Motion Picture "Annie")

Lyric by MARTIN CHARNIN
Music by CHARLES STROUSE

LET'S DO SOMETHING CHEAP AND SUPERFICIAL

Words and Music by
RICHARD E. LEVINSON

LET THE GOOD TIMES ROLL

Words and Music by SAM THEARD
& FLEECIE MOORE

LOVELIER THAN EVER
(From "Where's Charley?")

By FRANK LOESSER

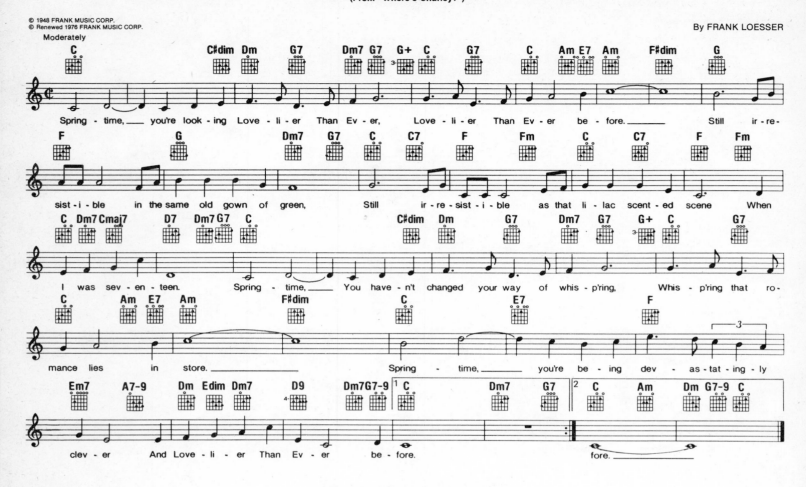

LULLABY OF THE LEAVES

Words by JOE YOUNG
Music by BERNICE PETKERE

MAGNETO AND TITANIUM MAN

Words and Music by
McCARTNEY

MAKING LOVE
(Theme Song)

Words and Music by CAROLE BAYER SAGER,
BURT BACHARACH & BRUCE ROBERTS

MAHOGANY HALL STOMP

By SPENCER WILLIAMS

MOUNTAIN OF LOVE

Words and Music by
HAROLD DORMAN

Moderately Slow

Standing on a mountain looking down on a city, the way I feel is a dog-gone pity. Tear-drops falling down a
Way down below there's a half million people, somewhere there's a church with a big tall steeple. Inside the church, there's an

moun-tain-side. Many times I've been here, Many times I've cried. We used to be so happy, when we were in love,
altar filled with flowers. Wedding bells are ringing and they should have been ours. That's why I'm so lonely my dreams gone above

high on a Mountain Of Love. Night after night, I've been standing here alone, weeping my heart out 'til the

cold gray dawn, praying that you're lonely and you'll come here too, hoping just by chance that I'll get a glimpse of you.

Trying hard to find you, somewhere above high on a Mountain Of Love. A Mountain Of Love, a Mountain Of Love.

D.C. al Coda

CODA

You should be ashamed, we used to be a Mountain Of Love but you just changed your name.

MAKE LOVE TO ME

Lyric by BILL NORVAS & ALLAN COPELAND
Music by LEON ROPPOLO, PAUL MARES, BENNY POLLACK,
GEORGE BRUNIES, MEL STITZEL & WALTER MELROSE

MAMAN
(From the Musical Production "Mata Hari")

Lyric by MARTIN CHARNIN
Music by EDWARD THOMAS

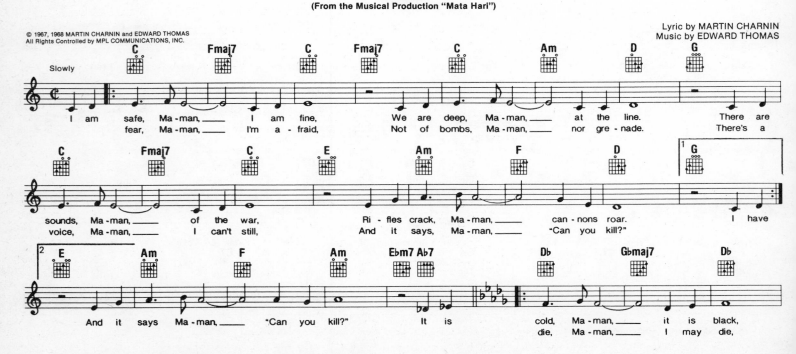

MAYBE
(From the Musical Production "Annie")

Lyric by MARTIN CHARNIN
Music by CHARLES STROUSE

MAME
(From the Musical Production "Mame")

Music and Lyric by
JERRY HERMAN

THE MAN THAT GOT AWAY
(From the Motion Picture "A Star Is Born")

Lyric by IRA GERSHWIN
Music by HAROLD ARLEN

MEMPHIS IN JUNE
(From the Motion Picture "Johnny Angel")

Lyric by PAUL FRANCIS WEBSTER
Music by HOAGY CARMICHAEL

THE MAPLE LEAF FOREVER

By ALEXANDER MUIR

MARY HAD A LITTLE LAMB

Words and Music by
McCARTNEY

you know," the teach-er did re-ply. And you could hear_ them sing-ing: La la, La la, La la la la la la

la. La la, La la la la, La la la la la. La la,_ La la,_ La la_ la.

MISERY AND GIN

Words and Music by
JOHN DURRILL & SNUFF GARRETT

Moderately

Mem-o-ries and drinks don't mix too well, and juke-box rec-ords don't play those wed-ding bells; ___

Look-in' at the world through the bot-tom of a glass, all I see is a man who's fad-in' fast. To-

night I need that wom-an a-gain.__ What I'd give for my ba-by to just_ walk in; _____

Sit down be-side me and say it's al-right, take me home and make sweet love to me _____ to-night. But

here I am a-gain_ mix-in' Mis-er-y_ And Gin, sit-tin' with all_ my friends and talk-in'_ to my-self; _ I

look like I'm hav-ing a good time _ but an-y fool _____ can tell that this hon-ky-tonk heav-en real-ly makes you

feel _____ like hell. I light a lone-ly wom-an's cig-a-rette _____ and

we start talk-in' a-bout what we wan-na for-get; _____ Her life sto-ry and mine_ are the same, we

both lost some-one and on-ly have our-selves to blame. But feel _____ like hell.

MAPLE LEAF RAG

Music by SCOTT JOPLIN
Revised Music and Lyrics by
JULE STYNE and BOB RUSSELL

Tempo di marcia

THE ME I NEVER KNEW
(From the Motion Picture "Alice's Adventures In Wonderland")

Lyric by DON BLACK
Music by JOHN BARRY

The me _____ I nev-er Knew _____ be-gan to stir _____ some-time this morn-ing. The me _____ I nev-er
Me _____ I Nev-er Knew _____ has learned to love _____ and love's the feel-ing. The Me _____ I Nev-er

Knew _____ ap-peared with-out _____ a word of warn-ing. You smiled _____ and you un-cov-ered what
Knew _____ can see a world _____ I've been con-ceal-ing To day _____ a new songs play-ing The

I _____ had not dis-cov-ered. You made _____ me see The Me _____ I Nev-er Knew. _____ The
words _____ one sim-ply say-ing from now _____ I'll be The Me _____ I Nev-er

Knew _____ From now _____ I'll be The Me _____ I Nev-er Knew. _____

MIGHTY OREGON

By DE WITT GILBERT
& ALBERT PERFECT

Or-e-gon, our Al-ma Ma-ter, We will guard thee on and on; _____ Fel-lows gath-er 'round and cheer her, _____ Chant her glo-ry, Or-e- gon. _____ Roar the prais-es of her war-riors, _____ Sing the sto-ry, Or-e-gon; _____ Down the grid-iron urge the he-roes, _____ Of our Might-y Or-e-gon. _____

MAY THE GOOD LORD BLESS AND KEEP YOU

Words and Music by
MEREDITH WILLSON

MEN OF PENNSYLVANIA

By CLAY BOLAND

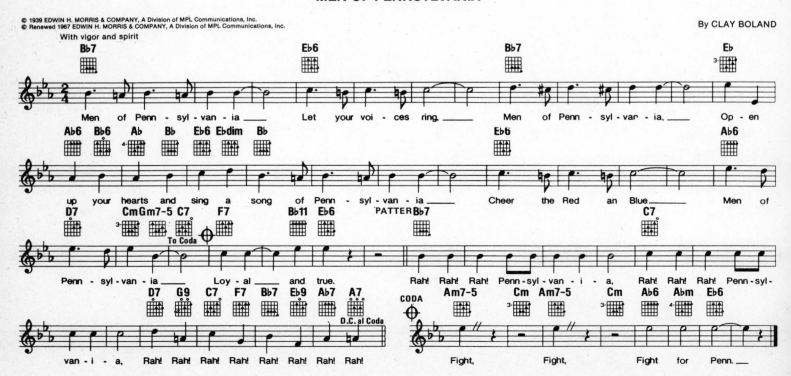

MAYBE BABY

Words and Music by
NORMAN PETTY & CHARLES HARDIN

MILENBERG JOYS

Words by WALTER MELROSE
Music by LEON ROPPOLO, PAUL MARES
& JELLY ROLL MORTON

THE MERRILY SONG (NO WHERE IN PARTICULAR)
(From the Motion Picture "The Adventures of Ichabod and Mr. Toad")

Lyric by LARRY MOREY & RAY GILBERT
Music by FRANK CHURCHILL
& CHARLES WOLCOTT

MIDNIGHT COWBOY
(From the Motion Picture "MIDNIGHT COWBOY")

Music by JOHN BARRY
Lyric by JACK GOLD

MEMORY

Text by TREVOR NUNN after T.S. ELIOT
Music by ANDREW LLOYD WEBBER

MIDNIGHT RODEO

MODERN GIRL

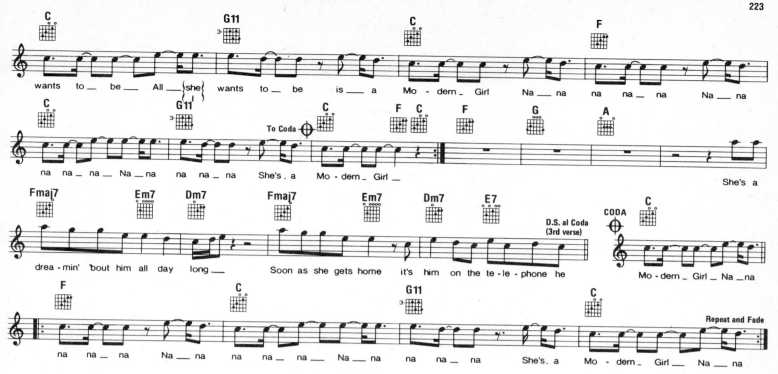

3. Asks her to dinner, she says she's not free
Tonight I'm gonna stay at home and
watch my T.V.

MOONLIGHT GAMBLER

Words by BOB HILLIARD
Music by PHILIP SPRINGER

MILK AND HONEY
(From the Broadway Musical "Milk And Honey")

Lyric and Music by
JERRY HERMAN

MISTER SANDMAN

Lyric and Music by
PAT BALLARD

THE MOON OF MANAKOORA
(From "The Hurricane")

Lyric by FRANK LOESSER
Music by ALFRED NEWMAN

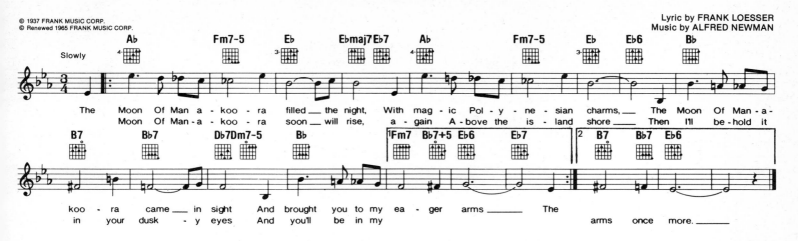

MORE I CANNOT WISH YOU
(From "Guys And Dolls")

By FRANK LOESSER

MOMMY, GIMME A DRINKA WATER!

By MILTON SCHAFER

MOONLIGHT BAY

Words by EDWARD MADDEN
Music by PERCY WENRICH

MORE LOVE THAN YOUR LOVE
(From the Musical Production "By The Beautiful Sea")

Words by DOROTHY FIELDS
Music by ARTHUR SCHWARTZ

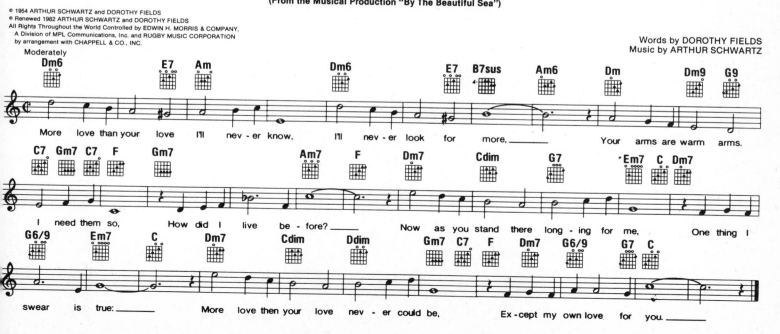

MORNING TRAIN (NINE TO FIVE)

Words and Music by
FLORRIE PALMER

MULL OF KINTYRE

Words and Music by
McCARTNEY

MORSE MOOSE AND THE GREY GOOSE

Words and Music by
McCARTNEY-LAINE

MUST IT BE LOVE?
(From the Musical Production "Bajour")

Music and Lyrics by
WALTER MARKS

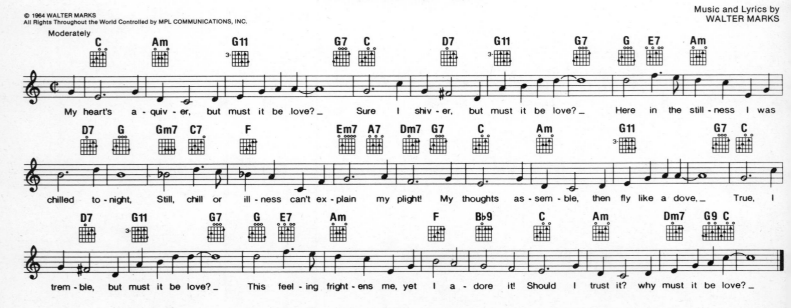

THE MUSIC AND THE MIRROR
(From the Musical Production "A Chorus Line")

Music by MARVIN HAMLISCH
Lyric by EDWARD KLEBAN

MORGEN

Words by MEL MANDEL & NORMAN SACHS
Music by PETER MOSSER

MY BEST GIRL (MY BEST BEAU)
(From the Musical Production "Mame")

Music and Lyric by
JERRY HERMAN

MUST DO SOMETHING ABOUT IT

Words and Music by
McCARTNEY

Moderately

I've just seen an-oth-er sun - set _ on my own. _ All day long _ I've been a-lone, _ and I

Must Do Some-thing A-bout It, yes I Must Do Some-thing A-bout It. Played an-oth-er los-ing card_
I've just seen an-oth-er sun-

game _ with my - self. _ Lone - ly jok - er on a shelf,
-set _ on my own. _ All _ day long _ I've been a-lone, _

and I Must Do Some-thing A-bout It, yes I Must Do Some-thing A-bout It. No one on the par-ty line,_
No one seems to need my vote,__

No one seems to need a dime, _ No one e - ven knows that I'm __ feel-ing this way. _
No one has to change a note, _ No one here to hold my coat, _ oh, what a day. _

I've just watched an-oth-er mov - ie _ on _ T. V. No - one's in _ the house_ but me, and I

Must Do Some-thing A-bout It, yes I Must Do Some-thing A-bout It. _____ Oh, _____ Oh, _____

some-thing a-bout _____ it. _____ I've just dialed an-oth-er num - ber_ on my phone._

All _ day long I've been a-lone, _ and I Must Do Some-thing A-bout It, yes I Must Do Some-thing A-bout It.

D.S. al Coda

CODA

Must Do Some-thing A-bout It, yes I Must Do Some-thing A-bout It.

MY DARLING, MY DARLING
(From "Where's Charley?")

By FRANK LOESSER

MY HEART BELONGS TO ME

Words and Music by
ALAN GORDON

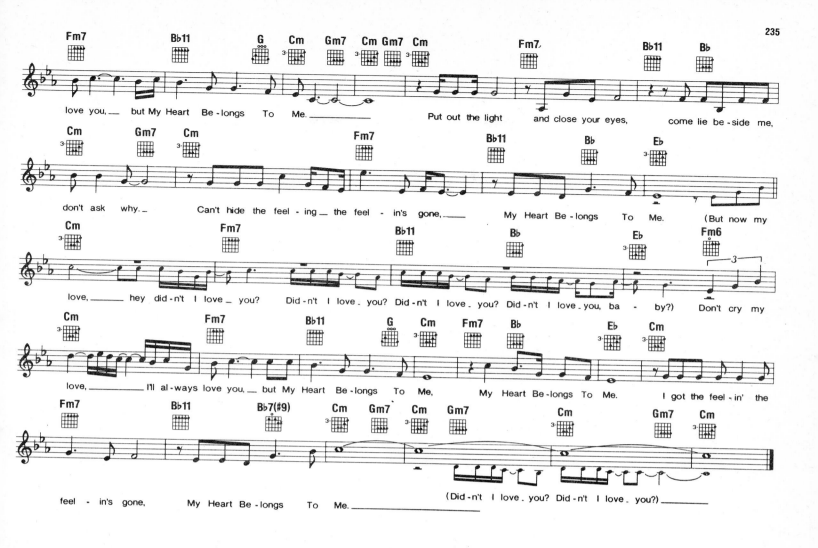

love you, __ but My Heart Be-longs To Me. __ Put out the light and close your eyes, come lie be-side me,

don't ask why. __ Can't hide the feel-ing __ the feel-in's gone, __ My Heart Be-longs To Me. (But now my

love, __ hey did-n't I love _ you? Did-n't I love _ you? Did-n't I love _ you? Did-n't I love _ you, ba-by?) Don't cry my

love, __ I'll al-ways love you, __ but My Heart Be-longs To Me, My Heart Be-longs To Me. I got the feel-in' the

feel-in's gone, My Heart Be-longs To Me. __ (Did-n't I love _ you? Did-n't I love _ you?) __

MY HEART IS SO FULL OF YOU
(From "The Most Happy Fella")

Broadly Romantic

By FRANK LOESSER

My Heart Is So Full Of You, so full of you. __ There is no room __ for an-y-thing more there.
My Heart Is So Full Of You, so full of you. __ There is no room __ for an-y-thing

more. __ What oth-er wish can I wish? What oth-er plan can I plan? What oth-er

dream can I dream, and what for? __ What-ev-er for? When My Heart Is So Full Of You, so

full of you __ There is no room, __ No room in my heart __ for an-y-thing more __

MY MAMMY

Words by SAM M. LEWIS & JOE YOUNG
Music by WALTER DONALDSON

MY LOVE

By PAUL McCARTNEY
& LINDA McCARTNEY

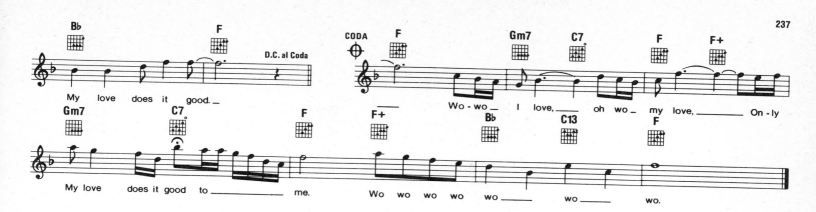

MY MAN BLUES

Words and Music by
BESSIE SMITH

MY ONE AND ONLY LOVE

Words by ROBERT MELLIN
Music by GUY WOOD

MY SHINING HOUR
(From the Motion Picture "The Sky's The Limit")

Lyric by JOHNNY MERCER
Music by HAROLD ARLEN

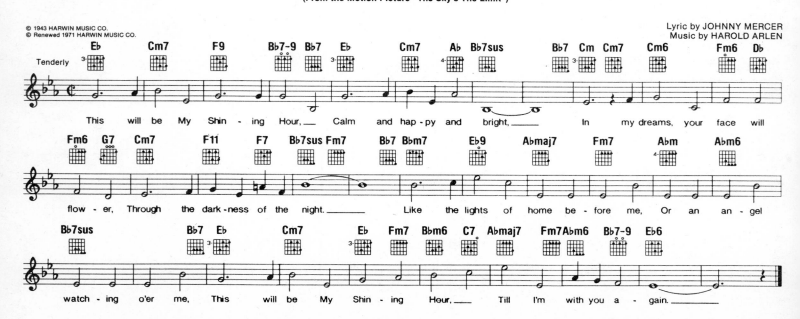

MY PA (MY LOVE)
(From "The Yearling")

Lyric by HERBERT MARTIN
Music by MICHAEL LEONARD

NEVER NEVER LAND
(From "Peter Pan")

Lyric by BETTY COMDEN & ADOLPH GREEN
Music by JULE STYNE

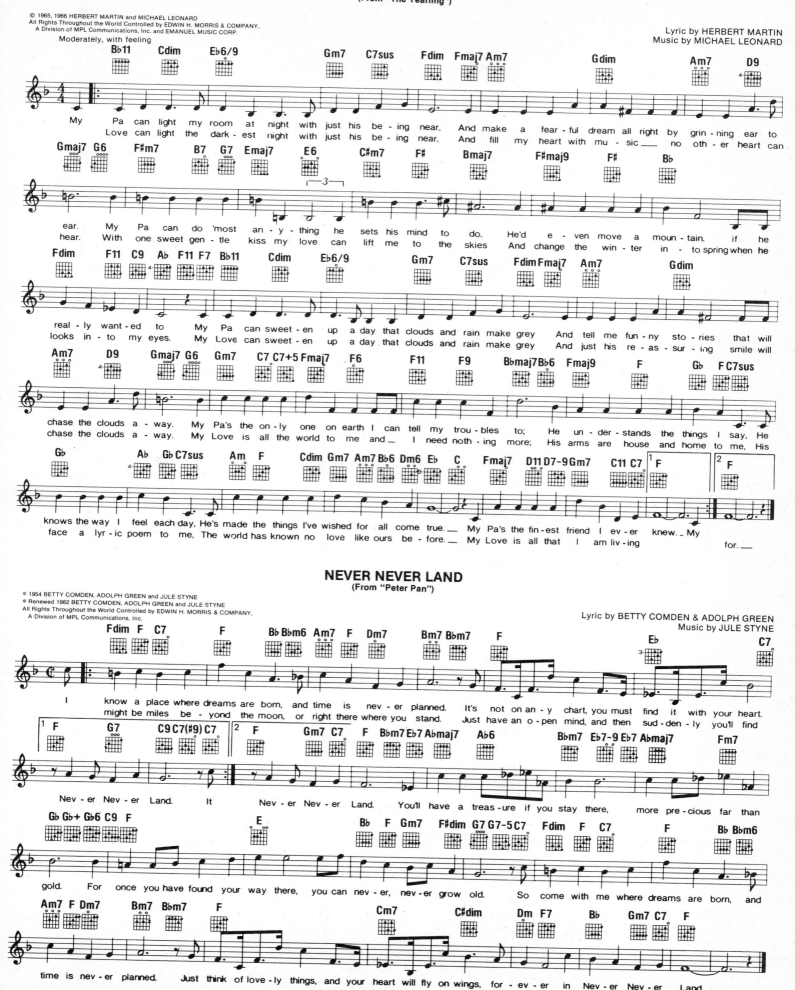

MY SON JOHN

Words by CAROLYN LEIGH
Music by SAMMY FAIN

NAVY BLUE AND GOLD

By J.W. Crosley

N.Y.C.
(FROM the Musical Production "Annie")

Lyric by MARTIN CHARNIN
Music by CHARLES STROUSE

NEVER WILL I MARRY
(From "Greenwillow")

By FRANK LOESSER

THE NIGHT IS YOUNG
(And You're So Beautiful)

Words by BILLY ROSE & IRVING KAHAL
Music by DANA SUESSE

NOBODY'S SWEETHEART

By GUS KAHN, ERNIE ERDMAN,
ELMER SCHOEBEL & BILLY MEYERS

NO WORDS
(For My Love)

Words and Music by
McCARTNEY-LAINE

NOTRE DAME VICTORY MARCH

Words by JOHN F. SHEA
Music by REV. MICHAEL J. SHEA

NINETEEN HUNDRED AND EIGHTY FIVE

Words and Music by
McCARTNEY

NELSON
(From "A Day In Hollywood")

Music and Lyric by
JERRY HERMAN

vo - cal chords car - ry in - sur - ance by Lloyd's and so, might I add, should his ad - e - noids. The lights wilt his hair - do on
pair made in heav - en," the fans love to say, but each time we kiss I swear that he's gay. In film af - ter film af - ter

cam - era he'll primp and quite frank - ly, his hair is - n't all that goes limp. Dar - ling Nel - son, how in - cred - i - bly
film I be - trothed him, we snug - gled and smooched, and oh God, how I loathed him. My Nel - son, oh so calm - ing you'll

bor - ing That's not sing - ing, it's snor - ing! What you're put - ting me through! _____
nev - er need en - balm - ing, Oh Nel - son,

A what you're put - ting me through! _____

NO MOON AT ALL

Words and Music by
REDD EVANS & DAVE MANN

No Moon At All _____ What a night, _ Ev - en light - nin' bugs have dimmed their light, _____ Stars have dis - ap peared from

sight and there's No _ Moon At All _____ Don't make a sound _ it's so dark, _ ev - en Fi - do is a -

fraid to bark, _ What a per - fect chance to park and there's No _ Moon At All, _____ Should we want at -

- mos - phere, _ for in - spir - a - tion, dear, _ One kiss will make _ it clear, _____ that to - night is right and bright moon - light might

in - ter - fere, _ No Moon At All _____ up a - bove, _ This is noth - ing like they told us of. _____

Just to think we fell in love and there's No _ Moon At All _____

NOTHING
(From the Musical Production "A Chorus Line")

Music by MARVIN HAMLISCH
Lyric by EDWARD KLEBAN

NOTRE DAME, OUR MOTHER
(A Song Of The University Of Notre Dame)

Words by REV. CHAS. L. O'CONNELL, C.S.C.
Music by JOSEPH J. CASASANTA

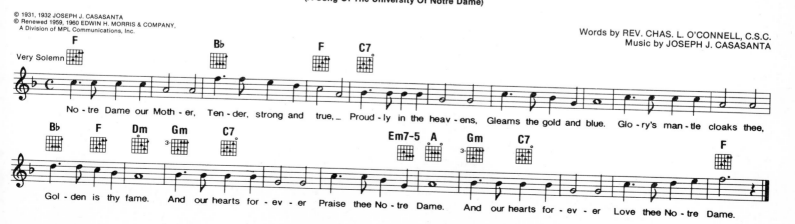

NEVER ON SUNDAY

Words by BILLY TOWNE
Music by MANOS HADJIDAKIS

Oh, you can kiss me on a Mon - day, a Mon - day, a Mon - day is ver - y, ver - y good.
cool day, a hot day, a wet day, which - ev - er one you choose.

Or you can kiss me on a Tues - day, a Tues - day, a Tues - day, in fact I wish you would.
Or try to kiss me on a gray day, a May day, a pay day, and see if I re - fuse.

Or you can kiss me on a Wednes - day, a Thurs - day, a Fri - day and Sat - ur - day is best.
And if you make it on a bleak day, a freak day, a week - day, why you can be my guest.

But Nev - er, Nev - er On A Sun - day, A Sun - day, A Sun - day, 'Cause that's my day of rest.
But Nev - er, Nev - er On A Sun - day, A Sun - day, the one day I need a lit - tle

Most an - y day you can be my guest, An - y day you say, but my day of rest. Just name the day

that you like the best, On - ly stay a - way on my day of rest. Oh, you can kiss me on a

rest.

THE NEW ASHMOLEAN MARCHING SOCIETY AND STUDENTS CONSERVATORY BAND
(From "Where's Charley?")

by FRANK LOESSER

March Tempo
VERSE

Here they come with the sun - light on the trum - pets
march on - ly slight - ly out of tem - po

Here they come with the ban - ners fly - ing
Though they play just a tri - fle out of

high In my throat I've a lump - y sort of feel - ing
tune Though there's just a sug - ges - tion in the o - boe

And the bright gleam of
Of the sound of a

pride is in my eye.
hound be - neath the moon.

Here they come with the clar - i - nets a - wail - ing
Though the trom - bone's a lit - tle in - de - pend - ent

Here they
And the

G7 **C6** **B7** **Em** **B7** **Em**

come rath-er brave-ly up the square _____ And I know in a mo-ment I'll be cheer-ing
drum-mer is not ex-act-ly choice _____ Still the old col-lege spir-it is up-on me

B7 **Em** **E7** **A** **C7** CHORUS **G** **G7** **C** **Cm6**

And my fine Sun-day hat will be high in the air for The { New Ash-mo-le-an
And I shout ev-'ry time at the top of my voice for The {

G **G7** **C** **Cm6** **G** **Am7** **D7** **G** **C**

March-ing So-ci-e-ty and Stu-dents Con-serv-a-to-ry band. _____ 1. Yes the New Ash-

C#dim **G** **E7** **A7** **D** **D7**

mo-le-an could have beat Na-po-le-on with all those dead-ly in-stru-ments in hand. There are
lyt-i-cal sen-si-tive or crit-i-cal you'll like it more the far-ther back you stand. But to

G **G7** **C** **Cm** **D7** **G** **A7** **D** **G** **G7**

those who fa-vor the phil-har-mon-ic fla-vor but to me the fin-est in the land _____ is The { New Ash-
me it's bul-ly it sat-is-fies me ful-ly when I hear that thun-der close at hand _____ from The {

C **Cm6** **G** **G7** **C** **Cm6** **G** **Am7** **D** 1 **G** 2 **G**

mo-le-an March-ing So-ci-e-ty and Stu-dents Con-serv-a-to-ry band. _____ 2. Though they band. _____
(To Verse)

OH BOY!

Words and Music by
SUNNY WEST, BILL TILGHMAN & NORMAN PETTY

Bright Tempo

G **C**

(1,3) All of my love, all of my kiss-in', You don't know what you been miss-in', Oh Boy! _ (Oh Boy!) When
(2) All of my life I been wait-in', To-night there'll be no hes-i-tat-in', Oh Boy! _

G **C#dim** **D7** 1 **G** **C** **D7** 2 **G** **C**

you're with me, _ Oh Boy! _ (Oh Boy!) The world can see _ that you were meant for me. me. _____
To Coda ⊕

G **D7** **G**

Stars ap-pear and shad-ows fall-in', You can hear my _ heart call-in', A

C **D7** **D7** CODA **G** **C6** **G** **C** **G**

lit-tle bit o' lov-in' makes ev-'ry-thing right, An' I'm gon-na see my ba-by to-ni-ght! me. _____
D.C. al Coda

NOT FADE AWAY

© 1957 MPL COMMUNICATIONS, INC. and WREN MUSIC CO.

Words and Music by
CHARLES HARDIN & NORMAN PETTY

NO TWO PEOPLE
(From "Hans Christian Andersen")

By FRANK LOESSER

© 1951, 1952 FRANK MUSIC CORP.
© Renewed 1979, 1980 FRANK MUSIC CORP.

OH BABY MINE
(I Get So Lonely)

Lryic and Music by
PAT BALLARD

OLD SIAM, SIR

Words and Music by
McCARTNEY

AN OCCASIONAL MAN
(From the Motion Picture "THE GIRL RUSH")

By HUGH MARTIN
& RALPH BLANE

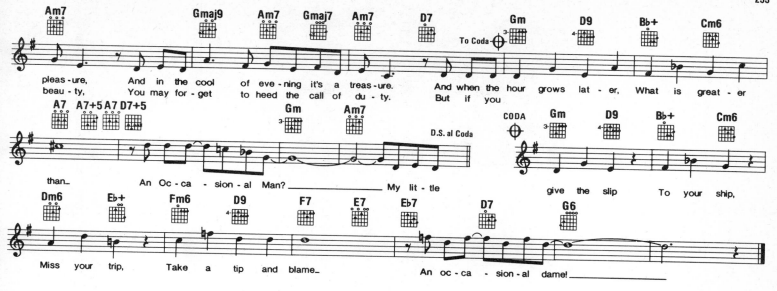

OLE BUTTERMILK SKY
(From the Motion Picture "Canyon Passage")

Words and Music by
HOAGY CARMICHAEL & JACK BROOKS

THE OLDEST ESTABLISHED
(From "Guys And Dolls")

By FRANK LOESSER

ON THE OTHER SIDE OF THE TRACKS
(From the Broadway Musical "Little Me")

Lyric by CAROLYN LEIGH
Music by CY COLEMAN

in-hi-bi-tions the axe; And to-mor-row morn-ing you'll find me, On The Oth-er Side_ Of The Tracks. On the oth-er side_ of that line,_ Where the life is fan-cy and free,_ Gon-na sit and fan_ on my fat di-van, While the but-ler but-tles the tea! But for now I'm fac-in' the fenc-es And I can't af-ford_ to re-lax; When the whole ka-boo-dle com-menc-es, On The Oth-er Side_ Of The Tracks. So I'm off and run-nin' o-ver the rail, I'm go'n' gun-nin' aft-er the quail! Off and run-nin', send_ me the mail, To the great big world on the oth-er side,_ The great big world on the far-ther side,_ The great big world On The Oth-er Side_ Of The Tracks!_____

ON WISCONSIN!

Words by CARL BECK
Music by W.T. PURDY

March

On, Wis-con-sin! On, Wis-con-sin! Plunge right thru that line!_____ Run that ball { clear 'round Chi-ca-go, / 'round Min-ne-so-ta, } A touch-down sure this time._____ On, Wis-con-sin! On, Wis-con-sin! Fight on for her fame!_____ Fight! fel-lows, Fight! And we will win this game._____ game._____

ON A SLOW BOAT TO CHINA

By FRANK LOESSER

ONE
(From "A Chorus Line")

Music by MARVIN HAMLISC
Lyric by EDWARD KLEBA

ON IOWA

Words and Music by
W.R. LAW

ONE BOY (GIRL)
(From the Musical Production "Bye Bye Birdie")

Words by LEE ADAMS
Music by CHARLES STROUSE

ONCE IN LOVE WITH AMY
(From "Where's Charley?")

By FRANK LOESSER

OPEN A NEW WINDOW
(From the Musical Production "Mame")

Music and Lyric
JERRY HERMAN

ON SECOND THOUGHT

Lyric by CAROLYN LEIGH
Music by CY COLEMAN

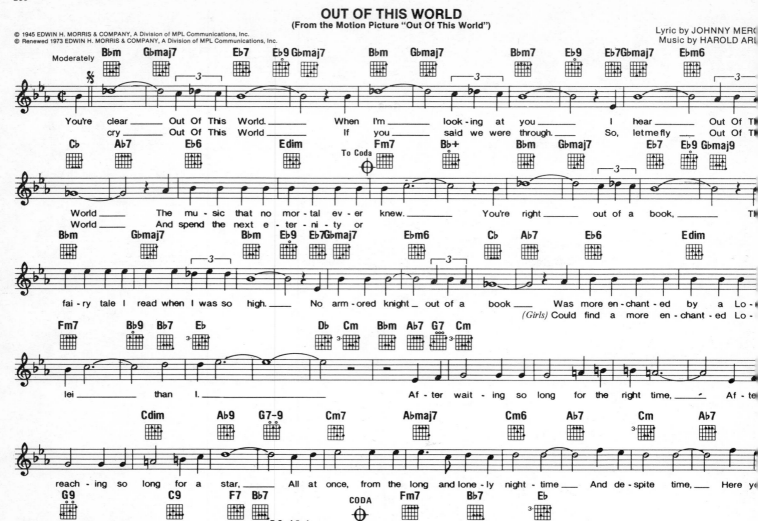

261

(Down At)
PAPA JOE'S

Words and Music by
JERRY SMITH

Moderately

wish you'd make the mu - sic dream - y and sad, _____ Could tell you a lot, ___ But you've got ___ to be
hope you did - n't mind my bend - ing your ear, _____ This torch that I've found, _ must be drowned or it

true to your code, _____ } Make it One For My Ba - by and one more for the road. You'd
might ex - plode, _____ }

nev - er know it, But Bud - dy, I'm a kind of po - et and I've got - ta lot - ta things to say, _____ And when I'm gloom - y, You

CODA

sim - ply got - ta lis - ten to me, Un - til it's talked a - way, ___ Well,   road, That long, long road. _____

There's a place in New Or - leans that serves fried chick - en with tur - nip greens, Craw - fish bisque that   treats you right and
Wait - ress comes to sit you down She's got the best frog legs in town, there's a wel - come sign hang - ing on the door so

Pa - pa Joe plays there ev - 'ry night, a lit - tle dark - haired beau - ty says "step right in" and you can bet a bo dol - lar she'll
don't you be a - fraid to ask for more, Now the on - ly time Joe clos - es at night is when the po - lice comes and turns

be yo' friend, ev - 'ry bod - y there has a tol - er - 'ble time down at Pa - pa Joe's, Oh the } food there is
out the light, they get a lit - tle mad but they don't fight down at Pa - pa Joe's, Oh the }

so de - li - cious, it melts right in yo' mouth.   and the mu - sic you hear is played by the

best band in the South   Pa - pa Joe's got a swing - ing band you can rock - 'n' - roll to
It's thick - er than fleas on a monk - ey's back but the folks down there, they

Dix - ie - land cus - tom - ers know it's the place to go, } Down at Pa - pa Joe's. ___ A lit - tle
like it like that, they live it up and they all come back }   Joe's.

PASS ME BY
(From the Motion Picture "FATHER GOOSE")

Lyric by CAROLYN LEIGH
Music by CY COLEMAN

"Swingy" march

I've got me ten fine toes to wig-gle in the sand. Lots of i-dle fin-gers snap to my com-
two great shoes that nev-er saw a shine. Trou-sers I can hold up with a laun-dry

mand. A live-ly pair of heels that kick to beat the band. Con-tem-plat-in' na-ture can be
line. A lov-e-ly patch that hides an aw-ful lot of spine. Shirt-tails cry-in' "Well, I'm a bloom-in'

fas-ci-nat-in'. Add to these a nose that I can thumb, And a mouth by gum have I,____
dan-de-li-on." Add to these a grin from ear to ear, And all the prop-er gear have I,____

____To tell the whole darn world if you don't hap-pen to like it deal me out, Thank you kind-ly Pass Me By.____
____To tell the whole darn world if you don't like the as-sort-ment deal me out, Thank you kind-ly Pass Me By.____ } Pass Me

By ____y, Pass Me By ____y ____y. If you don't hap-pen to like it Pass Me By.____ I've got me By.____

PALISADES PARK

Words and Music by
CHUCK BARRIS

Moderate twist

Last night I took a walk aft-er dark,_ A swing-in' place called Pal-i-sades Park;_ To have some fun and

see what I____ could see,____ That's where the girls are. I took a ride on the "Shoot-the-shoot",_

The girl I sat be-side was aw-ful cute;_ And when we stopped she was hold-in' hands_ with me,_

My heart was fly-in' Up a-like a rock-et-ship,____ Down a-like a roll-er-coast-er,

Fast a-like a "Loop-the-loop"_ And a-round a-like a mer-ry-go-round.____ We ate and ate at a

PARIS IS A LONELY TOWN
(From the Motion Picture "Gay Purr-ee")

Lyric by E.Y. HARBURG
Music by HAROLD ARLEN

P.S. I LOVE YOU

Words and Music by
JOHN LENNON & PAUL McCARTNEY

PECOS PROMENADE

Words and Music by LARRY COLLINS,
SANDY PINKARD & SNUFF GARRETT

PETTICOATS OF PORTUGAL
(Rapariga Do Portugal)

Words and Music by
MICHAEL DURSO, MEL MITCHELL
& MURL KAHN

PICASSO'S LAST WORDS
(Drink To Me)

Words and Music by
McCARTNEY

POOR SIDE OF TOWN

By JOHNNY RIVERS
& LOU ADLER

How can you tell ___ me   how much   you miss me? ___   When the last   time I
To him you were noth - ing   but a little   play thing, ___   Not much
So tell me: "Are you gonna stay, now?"   "Will you stand by

saw you ___   you would - n't e - ven kiss me? ___   That rich   guy you've been
more   than an ov - er - night fling.   To me   you were the
me   all the way now?   With you   by my

see - in' ___   must have put you   down;   So   wel - come   back   ba - by,
great - est thing ___   this boy had ev - er   found; ___   An' girl, it's hard   to   find   nice ___ things
side ___   they can't   keep us   down;   To - gether   we can   makeit   ba - by

to the Poor Side Of   Town. ___   I can't blame you for try - in'; ___   I'm try - in' to
on the Poor Side Of   Town. ___
on the Poor Side Of

make it, too.   I've got one lit - tle hang up, ba - by,   I just can't make it with - out you. ___   Town. ___

PUT ON A HAPPY FACE
(From the Musical Production "Bye Bye Birdie")

Words by LEE ADAMS
Music by CHARLES STROUSE

Gray skies are gon - na clear up, ___   Put On A Hap - py Face,   Brush off the clouds and cheer up, ___   Put On A Hap - py

Face.   Take off the gloom - y mask of trag - e - dy,   It's not your style;   You'll look so good that you'll be glad ya' de -

cid - ed to smile!   Pick out a pleas - ant out - look, ___   Stick out that no - ble chin;   Wipe off that "full of doubt" look, ___   Slap on a hap - py

grin!   And spread   sun - shine all o - ver the place,   Just Put On A Hap - py   Face! ___

PROMISES

Words and Music by
BARRY GIBB & ROBIN GIBB

PLAYBOY'S THEME
(From the Playboy Penthouse Party)

Lyric by CAROLYN LEIGH
Music by CY COLEMAN

So she's giv-ing him the razz-a-ma-taz-zle, And he's ob-vious-ly drink-ing it in;
So if you've been o-ver-heat-in' your ov-en, Just re-mem-ber that the boy is a Play-boy;

He's at-tract-ed to her du-bi-ous daz-zle, That's how it's been __ ev-er since sin. __
And the gal that makes a fire-side lov-in' man of the boy, __ Gets him to stay. __

Ev-'ry boy's a Play-boy, __ In __ his heart __ and soul. __

If __ your boy's a Play-boy, __ Loos-en your __ con-trol. __

If __ his eye me-an-ders, __ Sweet goose your gan-der's, __ Just one more or-ne-ry crit-ter, who

goes for the glit-ter.

CODA

Nev-er talks to him but sweet-ly, __ When he plays it in-dis-

creet-ly, __ Nev-er takes the play com-plete-ly __ a-way. __

PRISONER OF LOVE

Words and Music by
LEO ROBIN, CLARENCE GASKILL
& RUSS COLUMBO

A-lone from night to night, you'll find me, Too weak to break the chains that bind me; I need no shack-les to re-

mind me, I'm just a Pris-'ner Of Love. For one com-mand I stand and wait now, From one who's mas-ter of my

PUT ON YOUR SUNDAY CLOTHES
(From the Musical Production "Hello, Dolly!")

Music and Lyric by
JERRY HERMAN

PINE CONES AND HOLLY BERRIES
(From "Here's Love")

Words and Music by
MEREDITH WILLSON

RUBY, DON'T TAKE YOUR LOVE TO TOWN

Words and Music by
MEL TILLIS

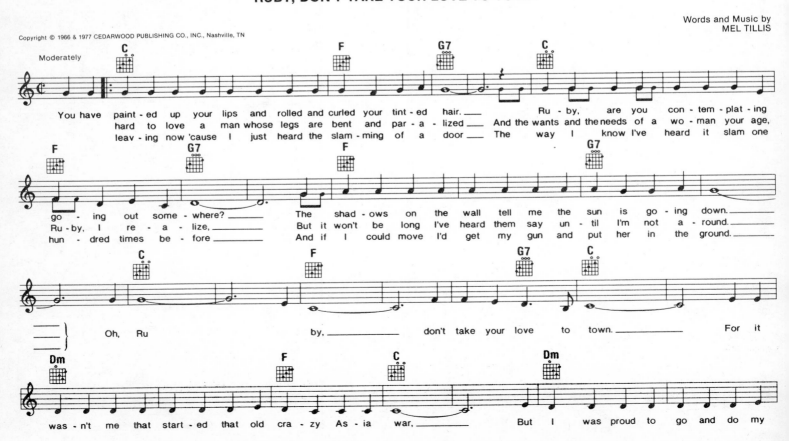

pa-tri-ot-ic chores. _____ Oh, I know, Ru-by, that I'm not the man I used to be,

_____ But, Ru by, _____ I still need your com-pa-ny.

It's
She's ny _____ for God's sake turn a-round, don't take your love to town. _____

PEGGY SUE

Words and Music by
JERRY ALLISON, NORMAN PETTY
& BUDDY HOLLY

If you knew _____ Peg - gy Sue, _____ Then you'd know why I feel blue _____ A-bout Peg - gy. _____
Peg - gy Sue, _____ Peg - gy Sue, _____ Oh, how my heart yearns for you, _____ Oh,Pa - heg - gy, _____

'Bout my Peg - gy Sue; _____ } Oh, well, I love you, gal, _____ Yes, I love you, Peg - gy Sue: _____
My Pa - heg - gy Sue; _____

Peg - gy Sue, _____ Peg - gy Sue, _____ Pret - ty, pret - ty, pret - ty, pret - ty, Peg - gy Sue, _____

_____ Oh, my Peg - gy, _____ My Peg - gy Sue; _____ Oh, well, I love you gal, _____

_____ and I need you, Peg - gy Sue. _____ I love you, _____ Peg - gy Sue, _____

With a love so rare and true, _____ Oh, Peg - gy, _____ My Peg - gy Sue; _____

Oh, well, I love you, gal, _____ Yes, I want you, Peg - gy Sue. _____

PHILADELPHIA FREEDOM

Copyright © 1975 by Big Pig Music Ltd.
Subpublished in the U.S.A. by Intersong-USA, Inc.

Words and Music by
ELTON JOHN & BERNIE TAUPIN

Verse 2. If you choose to, you can live your life alone
Some people choose the city,
Some others choose the good old family home

I like living easy without family ties
'Til the whippoorwill of freedom zapped me
Right between the eyes. (Repeat Chorus)

RAMBLING WRECK FROM GEORGIA TECH

By FRANK ROMAN

RAIN SOMETIMES

By ARTHUR HAMILTON

RECADO BOSSA NOVA

By LUIZ ANTONIO and DJALMA FERREIRA

Rave On

Words and Music by
SUNNY WEST, BILL TILGHMAN
& NORMAN PETTY

Bright Beat

The lit-tle things__you say and do,__ They make me want to be with you-hoo-hoo, Rave On! It's a cra-zy feel-in; and
way you dance__and hold me tight,__ The way you kiss and say good-ni - hi-hight,

I know it's__ got me reel-in' When you say, "I love_you,"_ Rave On.____ Well,__ the On.____

RIDERS IN THE SKY
(A Cowboy Legend)

By STAN JONES

Briskly

An old cow poke went rid-ing out one dark and wind-y day,____ Up - on a ridge he rest-ed as he
brands were still on fire__ and their hooves wuz made of steel,____ Their horns wuz black and shin-y and their

went a - long his way,____ When all at once a might-y herd of red - eyed cows he saw A
hot breath he could feel,____ A bolt of fear went through him as they thun-dered thru the sky For he

plough - in' thru the rag - ged skies ____ And up a cloud-y draw. ____
saw the ri - ders com - in' hard ____ And he heard their mourn-ful cry.

Yi - pi - yi - ay, ____ Yi - pi - yi - o, ____ 1. The ghost herd
2. ghost Riders

in ____ the sky. 2. Their ghost herd in ____ the sky. ____
In ____ The Sky. ____ 3. Their

Ghost Rid - ers In The Sky. ____

3. Their faces gaunt their eyes were blurred and shirts all soaked with sweat,
They're ridin' hard to catch that herd but they ain't caught them yet,
'Cause they've got to ride forever on that range up in the sky
On horses snortin' fire As they ride on, hear their cry.
Yi-pi-yi-ay, Yi-pi-yi-o, The ghost Riders In The Sky.

4. As the riders loped on by him he heard one call his name,
"If you want to save your soul from hell a-ridin' on our range,
Then cowboy change your ways today or with us you will ride
A-try'n to catch the devil's herd Across these endless skies."
Yi-pi-yi-ay, Yi-pi-yi-o, the ghost herd in the sky. Ghost Riders In The Sky.

REAL LIVE GIRL
(From the Broadway Production "Little Me")

Lyric by CAROLYN LEIGH
Music by CY COLEMAN

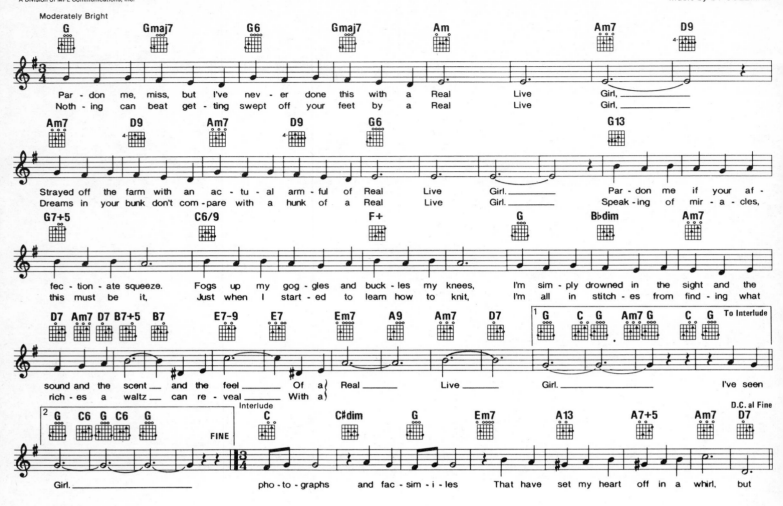

REBEL MARCH

Lyric by FRANCES WHITFIELD
Music by E.F. YERBY & R. ROY COATS

ROCCO'S THEME
(Far Away Land)
(From the Motion Picture "Rocco and His Brothers")

Words by MEL MANDEL & NORMAN SACHS
Music by NINO ROTA

ROSIE
(From the Musical Production "Bye Bye Birdie")

Words by LEE ADAMS
Music by CHARLES STROUSE

RIBBONS DOWN MY BACK
(From the Musical Production "Hello, Dolly!")

Music and Lyric by
JERRY HERMAN

ROUTE 66

By BOBBY TROUP

RED TOP

Words and Music by
LIONEL HAMPTON & BEN KYNARD

ROCKIN' CHAIR

Words and Music by HOAGY CARMICHAEL

ROCK SHOW

Words and Music by
McCARTNEY

k.

Be - hind the stacks_ you glimpse an axe. _____ The ten - sion mounts, you score an ounce, o-

le! Tem - p'ra - tures rise and you see the whites_of their eyes. _ If there's a Rock Show at the

Con - cert - ge - bow, _ you've got long hair at the Mad - i - son Square, they got Rock and Roll at the

Hol - ly - wood Bowl, _____ We'll be __ there,_ Oh, yeah!_

CODA

If there's a Rock Show at the Con - cert - ge - bow, _ They've got long hair at the

Mad - i - son Square_ You got Rock and Roll at the Hol - ly - wood Bowl_ If there's a Rock Show._

SAN

By LINDSAY McPHAIL
& WALTER MICHELS

Oh, sweet - heart Lo - na, My dar - ling Lo - na, Why have you gone a - way? _____

You said you loved me, But if you loved me Why did you act this way? _____

If I had ev - er been un - true to you What you have done would be the thing to do.

But my heart aches, dear, And it will break, dear, If you don't come back home a - gain to San.

ROCK-A-BYE YOUR BABY WITH A DIXIE MELODY

Words by SAM M. LEWIS & JOE YOUNG
Music by JEAN SCHWARTZ

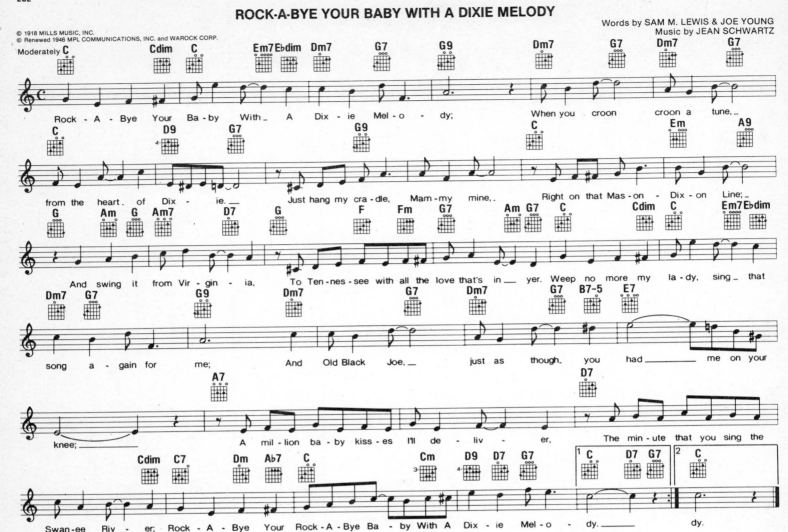

ROCKY TOP

Words and Music by
BOUDLEAUX BRYANT & FELICE BRYANT

3. I've had years of cramped-up city life
   Trapped like a duck in a pen;
   All I know is it's a pity life
   Can't be simple again. (Chorus)

THE RULES OF THE ROAD

Lyric by CAROLYN LEIGH
Music by CY COLEMAN

ROSETTA

Words and Music by
EARL HINES & HENRI WOOD

SAN FERNANDO VALLEY

Words and Music by
GORDON JENKINS

Oh! I'm pack-in' my grip And I'm leav-in' to-day, 'Cause I'm tak-in' a trip
I'll for-get my sins, I'll be mak-in' new friends Where the West be-gins

Cal - i - for - nia way. I'm gon-na set-tle down and nev-er more roam And make the San Fer-nan-do
And the sun-set ends, 'Cause I've de-cid-ed where "yours tru-ly" should be And it's the San Fer-nan-do

Val - ley my home.___ I think that I'm safe in stat-in' She will be wait-in' When my lone-ly
Val - ley for me.___

jour - ney is done ___ And kind-ly old Rev-'rend Thom-as Made us a prom-ise He will make the two of us

one. So, I'm hit-tin' the trail To the cow coun-try. You can for-ward my mail Care of R. F.

D. I'm gon-na set-tle down and nev-er more roam And make the San Fer-nan-do Val-ley my home.___

SEASIDE WOMAN

Words and Music by
McCARTNEY

1. Pa - pa catch the fish from the bot-tom of the sea, Ma-ma fix-es net, she keep an eye on me,
2. Ride grey mule to mar-ket - place each day, Sell the beads and bas-kets the sea shells pay,
3. Pa - pa catch the fish from the bot-tom of the sea, Ma-ma fix-es net, she keep an eye on me.

Dain - ty lit-tle ma-ma smile all day, Cook your sweet-po-ta-to, at night she lay,___ lay.
Dain - ty lit-tle ma-ma smile all day, Pa-pa love you ma-ma and he say,___ say:
Dain - ty lit-tle ma-ma smile all day, Pa-pa love you ma-ma, at night he lay,___ lay.

Oh, ___ Sea-side Wom-an. Oh, ___ Sea-side Wom-an.

1,2   3

Oh, ___ Sea-side Wom-an, Sea-side Wom-an.

SAN FERRY ANNE

Words and Music by
McCARTNEY

SENTIMENTAL JOURNEY

Words and Music by
BUD GREEN, LES BROWN & BEN HOMER

SALLY G

Words and Music by
McCARTNEY

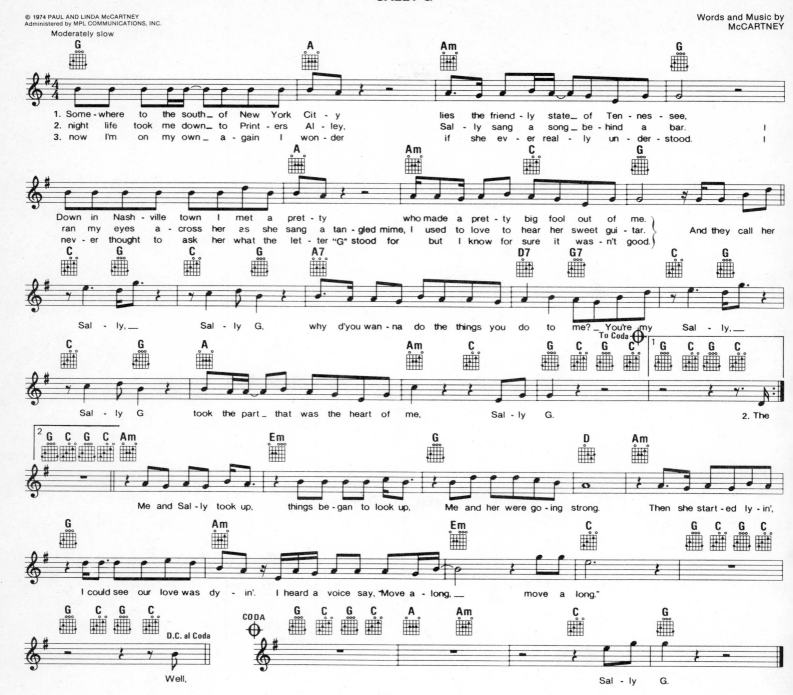

SATURDAY NIGHT FISH FRY

Words and Music by
ELLIS WALSH & LOUIS JORDAN

SANDY
(From The Motion Picture "Annie")

Lyric by MARTIN CHARNIN
Music by CHARLES STROUSE

SEVENTY SIX TROMBONES
(From "The Music Man")

By MEREDITH WILLSON

SHALOM
(From the Musical Production "Milk And Honey")

Music and Lyric by
JERRY HERMAN

SHE TOUCHED ME
(From the Broadway Musical "Drat! The Cat!")

Lyric by IRA LEVIN
Music by MILTON SCHAFER

SUE ME
(From "Guys And Dolls")

By FRANK LOESSER

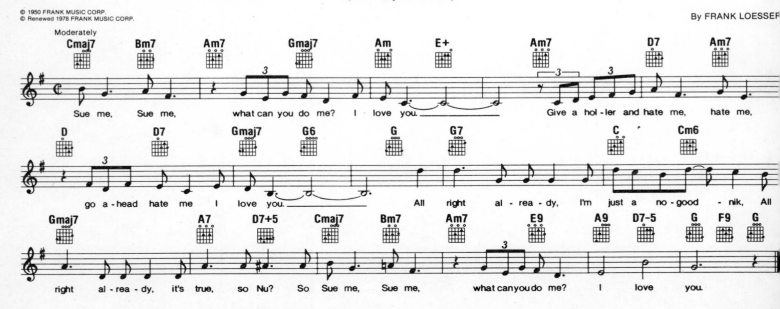

SIXTEEN CANDLES

Words and Music by
LUTHER DIXON & ALLYSON R. KHENT

SHOO-FLY PIE AND APPLE PAN DOWDY

Words by SAMMY GALLOP
Music by GUY WOOD

SINGLE PIGEON

Words and Music by
McCARTNEY

SHERRY

Words and Music by
BOB GAUDIO

Sher -ry ba -by, Sher -ry,___ can you come out to - night? Come, come, come out to - night.___

You _____ bet -ter ask your_ ma - ma, Sher -ry ba - by, Tell _____ her ___ ev -'ry -thing is all

right. Why don't you come on,_____ put your red dress on? _ Come on,_____ mm, you look so fine.

Come on,____ move it nice and eas - y, Girl,___ you make me lose my mind.___ Sher - ry - ba - by,

Sher -ry ba -by, Sher -ry,___can you come out to - night? Come, come, come out to -night._
Come, come, come out to - night._
Sher - ry, Sher -ry ba - by.

Repeat and Fade

SKYLARK

Lyric by JOHNNY MERCER
Music by HOAGY CARMICHAEL

Sky - lark _____ Have you an - y -thing to say to me?___ Won't you tell me where my love can be?_
Sky - lark _____ Have you seen a val - ley green with spring, _____ Where my heart can go a jour -ney - ing,

___ Is there a mea -dow in the mist, ___ Where some -one's wait -ing to be kissed?
___ O -ver the sha -dows and the rain, to a blos -som cov -ered lane? _ And in your

lone - ly flight, _____ Have -n't you heard the mu -sic in the night, _____ Won -der -ful mu -sic, Faint as a "will -o' the wisp,"

Craz - y as a loon, Sad as a gyp -sy ser -e - nad -ing the moon. Oh, Sky - lark, _____ I don't know if you can

find these things, _____ But my heart is rid -ing on your wings, _____ So, if you see them an - y -where, won't you lead me there?

SILLY LOVE SONGS

Words and Music by
McCARTNEY

SO LONG, DEARIE
(From the Musical Production "Hello, Dolly!")

Music and Lyric by
JERRY HERMAN

SHOULD I DO IT

Words and Music by
LAYNG MARTINE JR.

SIX O'CLOCK

Words and Music by
McCARTNEY

SIOUX CITY SUE

Lyric by RAY FREEDMAN
Music by DICK THOMAS

SIX LESSONS FROM MADAME LA ZONGA

Lyric by CHARLES NEWMAN
Music by JAMES V. MONACO

295

SIT DOWN YOU'RE ROCKIN' THE BOAT
(From "Guys And Dolls")

By FRANK LOESSER

SLAUGHTER ON TENTH AVENUE

Music by
RICHARD RODGERS

SOMEBODY BAD STOLE DE WEDDING BELL
(Who's Got De Ding Dong?)

Lyric by BOB HILLIARD
Music by DAVE MANN

Calypso beat

Some-bod - y bad stole de wed - ding bell! __ Some-bod - y bad stole de wed - ding bell! __ Some-bod - y bad stole de

wed - ding bell! __ Now no-bod - y can be mar - ried. Who's got de ding dong, who's got de bell? Who's got de ding dong,

who's got de bell? Some-bod - y know, but no-bod - y tell, 'cause some-bod - y bad stole de wed - ding bell! __ We got
We got
We got

sa's - 'pa - ril - la so - da on de ice, __ we got shoes and rice and free ad - vice. We got a
ver - y fine de - tec - tive, Sher - lock John, __ and he's sure to ques - tion ev - 'ry mon. __ Soon in de
so - los by de is - land's sing - ing band, __ we got lots of sun and lots of sand. __ We got a

bri - dal suite __ in hon - ey - moon ho - tel, __ but what good is that __ with - out a
mar - ket place __ where peo - ple buy and sell, __ he's sure to ar - rest __ de one who
lov - er's moon __ we got a wish - ing well, __ and oh, how I wish __ we had a

wed - ding bell! __
sells de bell! __   D.C. al Coda
wed - ding bell! __

CODA

No - bod - y tell 'cause some - bod - y bad _____ stole de wed - ding bell! _____

A SLEEPIN' BEE
(From "House Of Flowers")

Lyric by TRUMAN CAPOTE
& HAROLD ARLEN
Music by HAROLD ARLEN

SLEEPY LAGOON

Words by JACK LAWRENCE
Music by ERIC COATES

A SMILE WILL GO A LONG, LONG WAY

By Benny Davis
& Harry Akst

SNOWFLAKES AND SWEETHEARTS
From "I, Anastasia" (Based on themes of S. Rachmaninoff)

Music and Lyric by
ROBERT WRIGHT & GEORGE FORREST

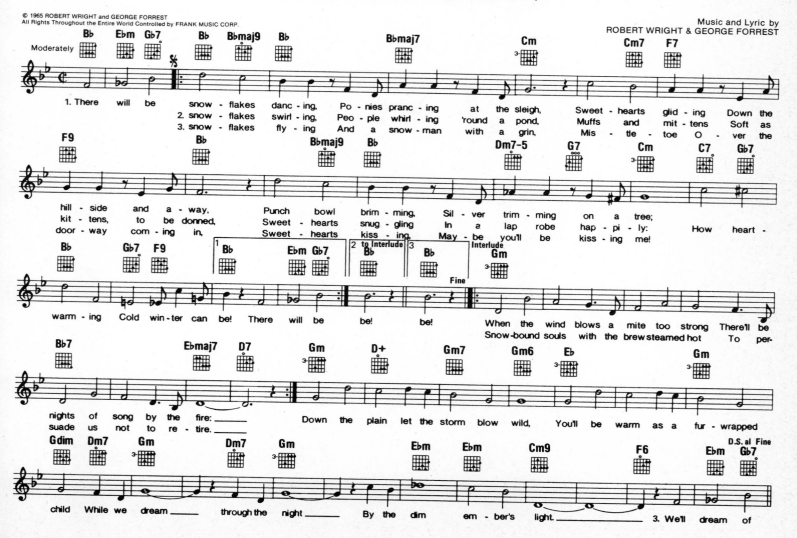

SNUG AS A BUG IN A RUG
(From the Motion Picture "THE GRACIE ALLEN MURDER CASE")

Words by FRANK LOESSER
Music by MATT MELNECK

SOMEBODY, SOMEWHERE
(From "The Most Happy Fella")

By FRANK LOESSER

SPIN IT ON

Words and Music by
McCARTNEY

Fast Rock

Spin it on, don't stop, take it back to the top 'cause I've ___ got an-oth-er lot of love for you. ___

I wan-na Spin It On, Spin It On. Off to the flicks with the pid-dle in her nix, to the / off to the field with a mis-sion-ar-y zeal for the

fair with her hair in curl-ers. Her cous-in could-n't get on down_ to the pleas-ure dome. Her cous-in had to / life of the wife of a farm-er. Her cous-in could-n't get on down_ to the vil-lage hall. Her cous-in had to

spend the night_ in an air-craft han-ger. Mem-o-ries._ Spin It On, don't stop, take it back to the top_ / spend the night_ on a pin-ball ta-ble. Mem-o-ries._ Spin It

'cause I've ___ got an-oth-er lot of love for you. _ That's why I wan-na Spin It

To Coda
On, Spin It On, Spin It On, Spin It On, don't stop, take it

back to the top ___ 'cause I've ___ got an-oth-er lot of love for you. _ That's

why I wan-na Spin It On.
D.S. al Coda
Well

CODA
Spin It On, Spin It

On. ___
I wan-na Spin It On, Spin It On.
D.S.S. and Fade
Spin It

SOMEBODY'S KNOCKIN'

Words and Music by
ED PENNEY & JERRY GILLESPIE

SONGBIRD

Words and Music by
STEVE NELSON & DAVID WOLFERT

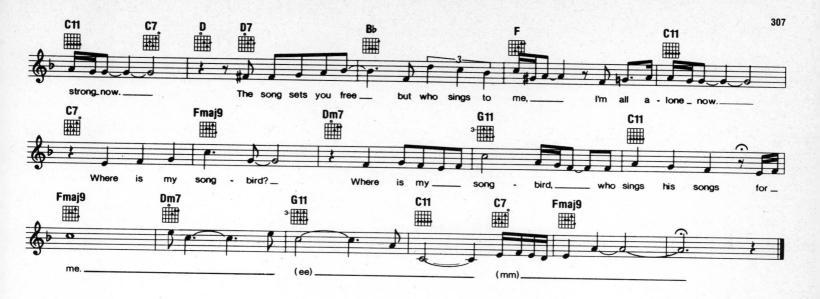

STANDING ON THE CORNER
(From "The Most Happy Fella")

By FRANK LOESSER

THE SONG OF NORWAY
(From the Motion Picture "Song Of Norway")

Based on "Piano Concerto in A Minor" by
EDVARD GRIEG
Lyric and Musical Adaptation by
ROBERT WRIGHT & GEORGE FORREST

In - form an un - know - ing world___ What we___ know well:___ That the land in the hard, cold north___ Has warm de - lights And soft mys - te - ries to tell!___ And then min - strel, You will have made a true song: The song of Nor - way, Whose mu - sic will ev - er en - shrine___ The heart___ of your be - lov - ed home___ and mine!___

SUNRISE SERENADE

Lyric by JACK LAWRENCE
Music by FRANKIE CARLE

Good morn - in', good morn - in' you sleep - y head,_ It's dawn - in', Stop yawn - in', Get out of that bed._ Say the air is soft as silk,_ it's time to get the morn - in' milk, Come on___ Wake up! Get up!___ Look at the grass___ sil - ver in the sun___ heav - y with the dew,___ Look at the buds___ you can al - most see_ how they're break - in' thru; Look at the birds_ feed - in' all their young_ in the sy - ca - mores___ But you bet - ter get on with your morn - in' chores.___ Just take a breath_ of that new mown hay_ and the su - gar cane;_ looks like to - night_ there should be a moon_ down in lov - er's lane.___ There you go day dream - ing when it's time that you o - beyed that Sun - rise Ser - e - nade._

S'POSIN'

Lyric by ANDY RAZAF
Music by PAUL DENNIKER

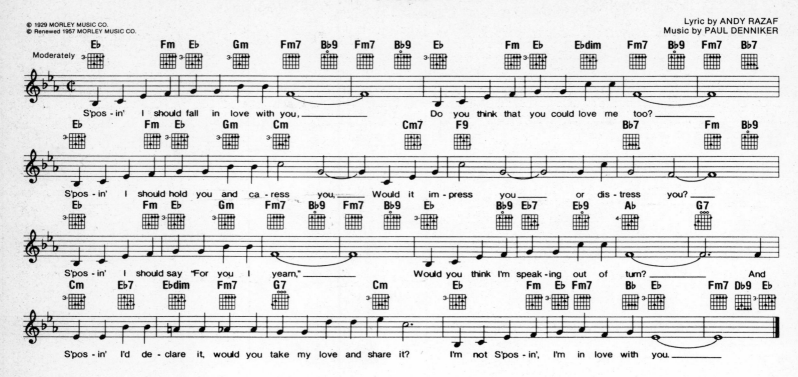

S'pos-in' I should fall in love with you,_____ Do you think that you could love me too?_____

S'pos-in' I should hold you and ca-ress you, Would it im-press you_____ or dis-tress you?

S'pos-in' I should say "For you I yearn," Would you think I'm speak-ing out of turn?_____ And

S'pos-in' I'd de-clare it, would you take my love and share it? I'm not S'pos-in', I'm in love with you._____

SOMEBODY WHO CARES

Words and Music by
McCARTNEY

When your bo-dy is com-ing a-part _ at the seams and the whole thing's feel-ing low, _ you're con-vin-cing your-self that there's

bo-dy has tak-en the wheels off your car, _ when you had some-where to go. _ Well it's an-noy-ing not go-ing to

no-bo-dy there, _ I _ know, I know how you feel _____ Like some-

get ve-ry far, _ I _ know, but some-bo-dy cares. _____ There's

al-ways some-one, _ some-where, you should know by now, _ al-ways Some-bo-dy Who Cares._ It's happ-'ning day in, _ day out,

well you know _ by now _ al-ways Some-bo-dy Who Cares._ If you don't know it, how will it find you,

how will we know _ your where-a-bouts? But I know how you feel. _ Like some-bo-dy has ta-ken the wheels off your car, _ when you

had some-where to go, _ well it's frus-tra-ting not go-ing to get ve-ry far _ I know _ but some-bod-y cares. _ There's

(I know) _

D.S. al Fine

Fine

SPRING WILL BE A LITTLE LATE THIS YEAR
(From "Christmas Holiday")

By FRANK LOESSER

STEPPIN' OUT

Words and Music by
BILLY STARR

STAY

Words and Music by
MAURICE WILLIAMS

Dance _____ just a lit-tle bit long-er, _____ Please, please, please, please tell _____ me that you're

go-in' to. _____ Now your dad-dy don't mind, _____ an your mom-my don't mind, _____ Could we

have an-oth-er dance, dear. _____ Just-a one more, one _____ more time. Oh, won't you Stay _____

_____ just a lit-tle bit long-er, _____ Please let me dance, _____ Please say that you will.

SUGAR

Words by JOE YOUNG
Music by GEORGE W. MEYER

(Male) Su - gar, I call my ba - by my Su - gar, I nev-er 'may-be' my Su - gar, That's why my ba - by is
(Female) Su - gar, I call my ba - by my Su - gar, I nev-er 'may-be' my Su - gar, That's why my ba - by is

so con-fec-tion-ar - y, Fun - ny, She nev-er pleads. for my mon - ey, But when she feeds. me on
so con-fec-tion-er - y, Fun - ny, I nev-er plead _ for his mon - ey, 'Cause when I feed _ him on

hon - ey, She gets her needs. ev-'ry time. _____ I'd make a mil-lion trips _ to her lips _ If I _ were a
hon - ey, I gets my needs. ev-'ry time. _____ I'd make a mil-lion trips _ to his lips _ If I _ were a

bee, 'Cause they are sweet-er than _ an-y can-dy to me, She's gran-u-lat - ed Sugar, I nev-er cheat_ on my
bee, 'Cause they are sweet-er than_ an-y can-dy to me, He's gran-u-lat - ed Sugar, I nev-er cheat_ on my

Su - gar, 'Cause I'm too sweet_ on my Su - gar, That Su-gar ba - by o' mine.
Su - gar, 'Cause I'm too sweet_ on my Su - gar, That Su-gar ba - by o' mine. _____

STOMPIN' AT THE SAVOY

Words and Music by
BENNY GOODMAN, ANDY RAZAF,
CHICK WEBB & EDGAR SAMPSON

STORMY WEATHER
(Keeps Rainin' All The Time)

Words by TED KOEHLER
Music by HAROLD ARLEN

SORRY SEEMS TO BE THE HARDEST WORD

Words and Music by
ELTON JOHN & BERNIE TAUPIN

STRICTLY INSTRUMENTAL

Words by EDDIE SEILER
Music by SOL MARCUS, BENNIE BENJAMIN
& EDGAR BATTLE

SMILE A LITTLE SMILE FOR ME

Words and Music by
TONY MACAULEY & GEOFF STEPHENS

SUMMER NIGHTS
(From "GREASE")

Lyric and Music by
WARREN CASEY & JIM JACOBS

SUPERMAN

Words and Music by
RICHIE SNYDER

SUMMER RAIN

Words and Music by
JAMES HENDRICKS

THE SWEETHEART OF SIGMA CHI

Words by BYRON D. STOKES
Music by F. DUDLEIGH VERNOR

Sugar Foot Stomp

Lyric by WALTER MELROSE
Music by JOE OLIVER

SWEETHEARTS ON PARADE

Words by CHARLES NEWMAN
Music by CARMEN LOMBARDO

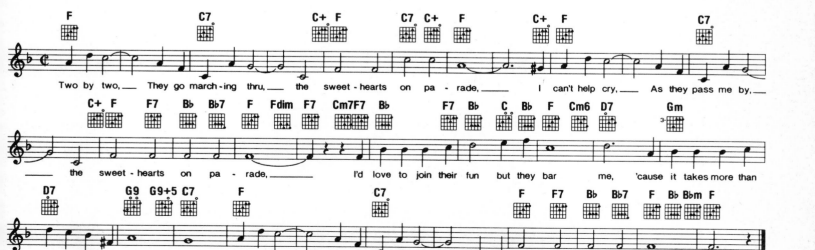

STILL DOIN' TIME

Words and Music by
MICHAEL P. HEENEY & JOHN E. MOFFAT

TIN ROOF BLUES

Words by WALTER MELROSE
Music by NEW ORLEANS RHYTHM KINGS

TILL THERE WAS YOU
(From "The Music Man")

By MEREDITH WILLSON

SIMILAU
(See-me-lo)

Words by HARRY COLEMAN
Music by ARDEN CLAR

TAKE BACK YOUR MINK
(From "Guys And Dolls")

By FRANK LOESSER

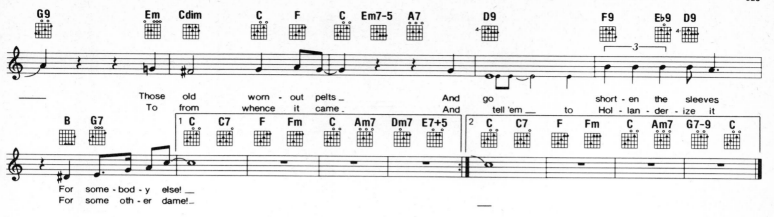

'TAIN'T WHAT YOU DO
(It's The Way That Cha Do It)

Words and Music by
SY OLIVER & JAMES YOUNG

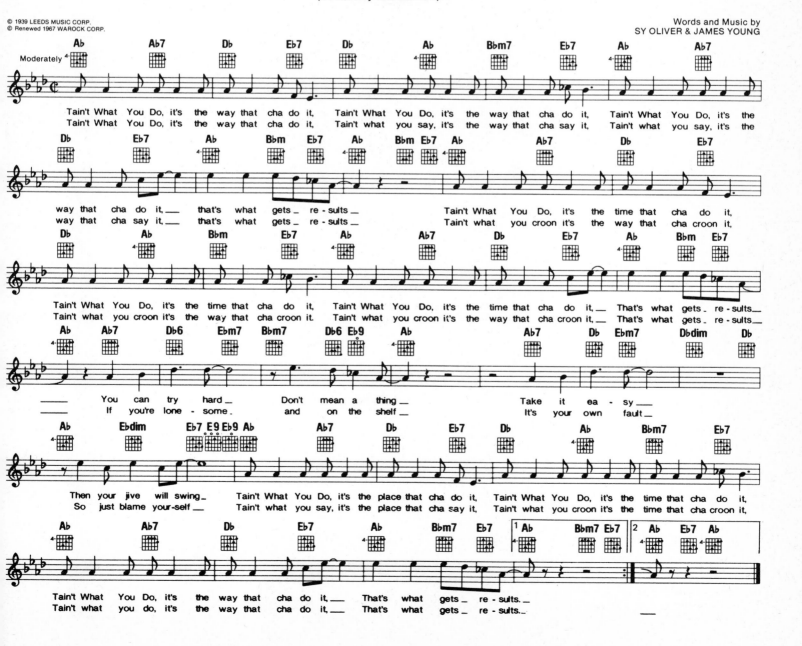

Someone Saved My Life Tonight

Words and Music by
ELTON JOHN & BERNIE TAUPIN

Verse 2. I never realised the passing hours
Of evening showers,
A slip noose hanging in my darkest dreams.
I'm strangled by your haunted social scene
Just a pawn out-played by a dominating queen.

It's four-o-clock in the morning
Damn it!
Listen to me good.
I'm sleeping with myself tonight
Saved in time, thank God my music's still alive. To Chorus.

TEMPORARY SECRETARY

Words and Music by
McCARTNEY

TALLAHASSEE LASSIE

Words and Music by
FRANK C. SLAY, JR., BOB CREWE
& FREDERICK A. PISCARIELLO

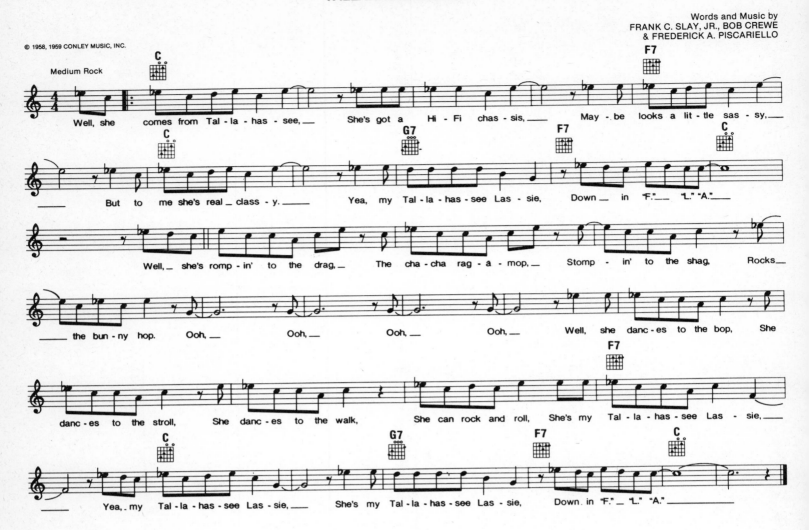

TALL HOPE
(From the Musical Production "Wildcat")

Lyric by CAROLYN LEIGH
Music by CY COLEMAN

THAT FACE

Lyric by ALAN BERGMAN & LEW SPENCE
Music by LEW SPENCE

TENDERLY

Lyric by JACK LAWRENCE
Music by WALTER GROSS

THEY WERE DOIN' THE MAMBO

Words and Music by
SONNY BURKE & DON RAYE

TEXAS IN MY REAR VIEW MIRROR

Words and Music by
MAC DAVIS

la-dy in red __ who danced in my dreams __ as I tossed in __ bed __ I knew I'd wind __ up __ in

jail or dead __ if I had to stay __ I thought hap-pi-ness was Lub-bock Te-

CHORUS

__ xas In My Rear View Mir-ror __ My ma-ma kept call-in' me home but I __ just __ did __

To Coda

__ not wan-na hear her and the vi-sion __ was get-tin' __ clear-er in my dreams __

so But the Hol-ly-wood moon did-n't smile __ the same old smile that I'd grown up __

__ with And the la-dy in red just want-ed __ my last __ dime __ And I

cried my-self to sleep __ at night __ too dumb to run too scared to fight __ and

D.S. with V.3 & 1st end.
then D.S. with V.4 al Coda

CODA

too proud __ to ad-mit it at __ the time __ So I And I

think I fi-nal-ly know __ just what it means __ And when I die __ you can

Fine

bur-y me in Lub-bock Te-xas __ in my jeans __

VERSE 2
So I lit out one night in June
Stoned on the glow of the Texas moon
Hummin' an old Buddy Holly tune called "Peggy Sue"
With my favorite jeans and a cheap guitar
I ran off chasing a distant star
If Buddy Holly could make it that far then
I figured I could too. (CHORUS)

VERSE 3
So I got me some gigs on Saturday nights
Not much more than orchestrated fights
And I'd come home drunk and try to write
But the words came out wrong
Hell-bent and bound for a wasted youth
Too much gin and not enough vermouth
And no one to teach me how to seek the truth
Before I put it in a song. (CHORUS)

VERSE 4
Well I thank God each and every day
For giving me the music and the words to say
'Cause I'd have never made it any other way
He was my only friend
And now I sleep a little better at night
And when I look in the mirror in the mornin' light
The man I see was both wrong and right
And he can go home again.

(Last time only)
CHORUS 2
Happiness was Lubbock, Texas In My Rear View Mirror
But now happiness is Lubbock, Texas
Growin' nearer and dearer
And the vision's gettin' clearer in my dreams
And I finally know just what it means
And when I die you can bury me
In Lubbock, Texas in my jeans.

THAT'LL BE THE DAY

Words and Music by
NORMAN PETTY, BUDDY HOLLY
& JERRY ALLISON

Well, you give me all your lov - in' and your tur - tle-dov - in,' All __ your hugs an' kiss - es an' your

mon - ey too; __ Well, you know you love me, ba - by, Un - til you tell me, may - be, that some day, well,

I'll be through! Well, __ That - 'll Be The Day, when you say, good - bye, Yes, __ That - 'll Be The Day, when

you make me cry, Ah, you say you're gon - na leave, you know it's a lie, __ 'cause That - 'll Be The Day __

__ when I die. __ Well, __ when I die. __ When Cu - pid shot his dart, He shot it at your heart,

So if we ev - er part and I leave you, You say you told me an' you told me bold - ly, That some day, well, I'll be through. Well,

THIS IS MY COUNTRY

Words by DON RAYE
Music by AL JACOBS

This Is My Coun - try! Land of my birth. __ Land of my choice. __ This Is My Coun - try!

Grand - est on earth! __
Hear my proud voice! __ I pledge thee my al - le - giance, A - mer - i - ca __ the bold. __ For

This Is My Coun - try, to have and to hold! hold! __

THERE WILL NEVER BE ANOTHER YOU
(From the Motion Picture "ICELAND")

Music by HARRY WARREN
Lyric by MACK GORDON

TIME HEALS EVERYTHING

Music & Lyric by
JERRY HERMAN

THUMBELINA
(From "Hans Christian Andersen")

By FRANK LOESSER

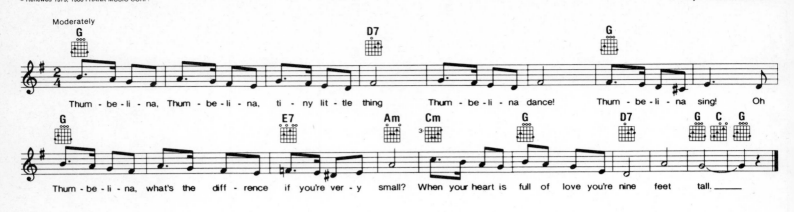

TREAT HER GENTLY — LONELY OLD PEOPLE

Words and Music by
McCARTNEY

TODAY I LOVE EV'RYBODY
(From the Motion Picture "The Farmer Takes A Wife")

Lyric by DOROTHY FIELDS
Music by HAROLD ARLEN

TRUE LOVE WAYS

Words and Music by
NORMAN PETTY & BUDDY HOLLY

TOMORROW
(From "Annie")

Lyric by MARTIN CHARNIN
Music by CHARLES STROUSE

The sun-'ll come out ___ To-mor-row, bet your bot-tom dol-lar that To-mor-row ___ there'll be sun! Jus'

think-ing a-bout ___ To-mor-row clears a-way the cob-webs and the sor-row ___ till there's none. When I'm stuck with a

day that's gray and lone-ly, ___ I just stick out my chin and grin and say: ___ Oh! The

sun-'ll come out ___ To-mor-row, So you got to hang on till To-mor-row ___ come what

may! To-mor-row, To-mor-row, I love ya To-mor-row, you're al-ways a day a-way! ___

TUNES OF GLORY
(From the Motion Picture "Tunes of Glory")

Words by MEL MANDEL & NORMAN SACHS
Music by MALCOLM ARNOLD

We are the Tunes Of Glo-ry! We tell the Free-dom Sto-ry! We are the tunes that men of peace took to
We flew with bom-bar-diers, We rode with the en-gin-eers, We walked with the in-fan-try that wad-ed a-

war! Proud as can be, to be, the mus-ic of li-ber-ty that march-es with ev-'ry fife and drum bug-le
shore! We sailed to Nor-man-dy! We marched on to Ger-man-y! We stepped on the goose-step as we did once be-

corps! We fought at Lex-ing-ton, there with the mus-ket-gun! We in-spired the heart of Wash-ing-ton! We are the
fore! Long live de-mo-cra-cy! Down, down with tyr-an-ny! Free men fight for a cause they know is right! Sing of the

Tunes Of Glo-ry! We tell the Free-dom Sto-ry! Dun-kirk, Cor-re-gi-dor, and so man-y more! ___
na-tion's pride and sing of the men who died to make sure the Tunes Of Glo-ry live ev-er more! ___

TUG OF WAR

Words and Music by
McCARTNEY

TWO LADIES IN DE SHADE OF DE BANANA TREE
(From "House Of Flowers")

Lyric by TRUMAN CAPOTE & HAROLD ARLEN
Music by HAROLD ARLEN

Moderately

When you fly-in' too high, like birds sweep-in' de sky, an' pulse makes you to pause, the main
With lips pout-in' to please, an' eyes rol-lin' to tease, the most pop-u-lar plan de-signed

rea-son and cause two la-dies in de shade of de ba-na-na tree. __ How de-lec-ta-ble, de-sir-ous
to cap-ture man, Two la-dies in de shade of de ba-na-na tree. __ What a fro-lick-in' spec-ta-cle

they can be, _ in de black, black shade of de ba-na-na tree. _____
they can be, _ In de ice-cold shade of de ba-na-na tree. __ De nights, they al-ways

fair, no-bod-y nev-er wear a stitch too much from here to here, or ev-en there to there. A man's

for-tu-nate chile to be born on this el-e-gan' isle. You need no wed-ded wife. _ To taste the joys of life. _ Look?

See? Nice? _ A-gree? Two la-dies in de shade of de ba-na-na tree. _____

A TEXAS STATE OF MIND

Words and Music by CLIFF CROFFORD,
JOHN DURRILL & SNUFF GARRETT

Medium Country Blues

I'm in a Tex-as ___ State Of Mind ___ Been gone way too long ___ this time _____ Cal-i-for-nia's too damn far from

you and that _ old lone star _ I'm in a Tex-as State _ Of _ Mind Your dreams are much more than _ mine and each

TRAGEDY

Words and Music by
GERALD H. NELSON & FRED B. BURCH

TWO LOST SOULS
(From "Damn Yankees")

Words and Music by
RICHARD ADLER & JERRY ROSS

Moderately Slow, with a heavy beat

Two Lost Souls on the high-way of life, We ain't e-ven got a sis-ter or broth-er,___ But
Two lost ships on a storm-y sea, One with no sail and one with no rud-der,___ But

ain't it just great, ain't it just grand? We've got each oth-er!___
ain't it just great, ain't it just grand? We've got each oth-er!___ Two lost sheep, in the

wilds of the hills, Far from the oth-er Jacks and Jills, We wan-dered a-way and went a-stray, But

we ain't fuss-in', cuz we've got "us 'n." We're Two Lost Souls on the high-way of life And there is no one with

whom we would "ruth-er,"___ Say, "Ain't it just great, ain't it just grand? We've got each oth-er!"___

Mom-ma said, "no," so we e-loped and though we ain't got the cas-tle for which we hoped, We've got a

lot, Be-cuz we've got each oth-er!_____

THERE ARE DAYS AND THERE ARE DAYS
(From the Broadway Musical "The First")

Lyric by MARTIN CHARNIN
Music by BOB BRUSH

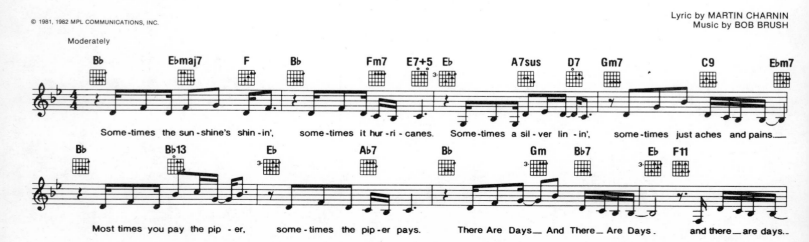

Moderately

Some-times the sun-shine's shin-in', some-times it hur-ri-canes. Some-times a sil-ver lin-in', some-times just aches and pains.___

Most times you pay the pip-er, some-times the pip-er pays. There Are Days___ And There___ Are Days. and there___ are days.

TOO YOUNG

Words by SYLVIA DEE
Music by SID LIPPMAN

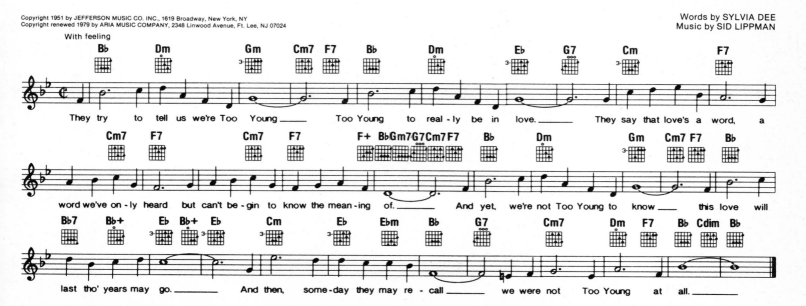

TUXEDO JUNCTION

Words by BUDDY FEYNE
Music by ERSKINE HAWKINS, WILLIAM JOHNSON
& JULIAN DASH

THE TWELFTH OF NEVER

Lyric by PAUL FRANCIS WEBSTER
Music by JERRY LIVINGSTON

TWO HEARTS IN THREE-QUARTER TIME

Words and Music by
J. YOUNG, R. STOLZ,
W. REISCH & A. ROBINSON

Two hearts beat with a joy com-plete, Oh, what a night for you and for me! Two hearts beat with a love so sweet, While waltz-ing dream-i-ly, _____ I'll share your charms till the break of the dawn, Locked in your arms till the new day is born. Two Hearts beat with a joy com-plete, Waltz-ing to a new par-a-dise. Two

TWO TICKETS TO GEORGIA

Words and Music by
JOE YOUNG, CHARLES TOBIAS
& J. FRED COOTS

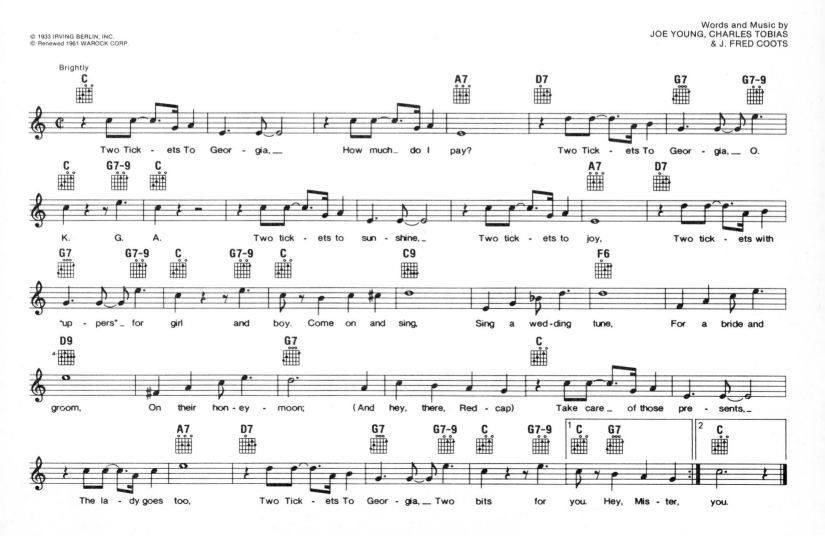

Two Tick-ets To Geor-gia, _ How much_ do I pay? Two Tick-ets To Geor-gia, _ O. K. G. A. Two tick-ets to sun-shine, _ Two tick-ets to joy, Two tick-ets with "up-pers" _ for girl and boy. Come on and sing, Sing a wed-ding tune, For a bride and groom, On their hon-ey-moon; (And hey, there, Red-cap) Take care _ of those pre-sents, _ The la-dy goes too, Two Tick-ets To Geor-gia, _ Two bits for you. Hey, Mis-ter, you.

TAKE IT AWAY

Words and Music by
McCARTNEY

THROUGH THE YEARS

Words and Music by
STEVE DORFF & MARTY PANZER

THE U. OF M. ROUSER

Words and Music by
FLOYD M. HUTSELL

UP, UP AND AWAY

Words and Music by
JIM WEBB

UNCLE ALBERT/ADMIRAL HALSEY

Words and Music by
McCARTNEY

UNCHAINED MELODY
(From "Unchained")

Lyric by HY ZARET
Music by ALEX NORTH

WALK LIKE A MAN

Words and Music by
BOB CREWE & BOB GAUDIO

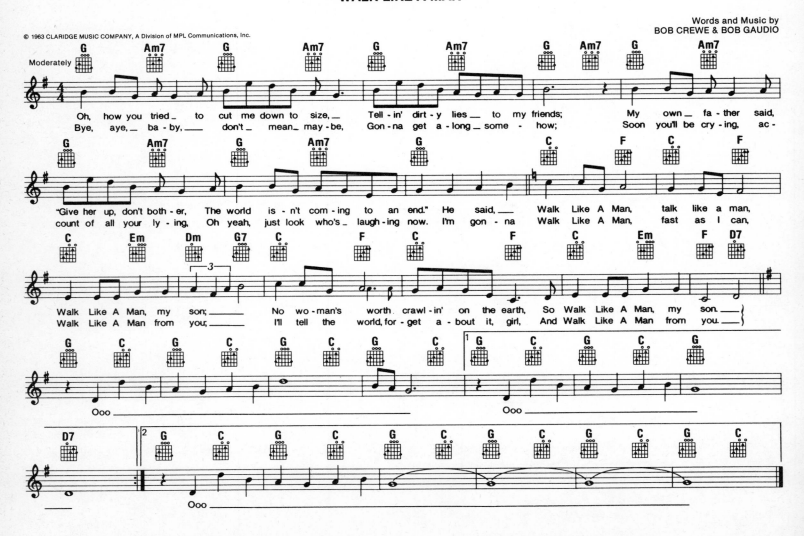

UP WITH THE WHITE AND GOLD

By FRANK ROMAN

WARM AND BEAUTIFUL

Words and Music by
McCARTNEY

VENUS AND MARS

Words and Music by
McCARTNEY

VIOLETS AND SILVERBELLS
(From the Musical Production "Shenandoah")

Lyric by PETER UDELL
Music by GARY GELD

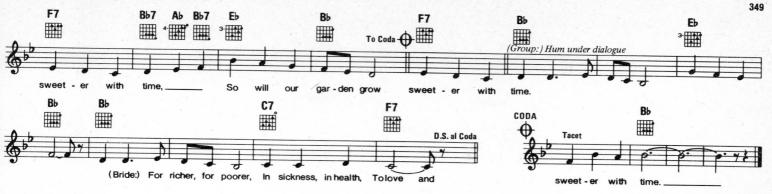

sweet-er with time, _____ So will our gar-den grow sweet-er with time.

(Group:) *Hum under dialogue*

(Bride:) For richer, for poorer, In sickness, in health, To love and

CODA *Tacet*

sweet-er with time. _____

THE VICTORS

By LOUIS ELBEL

Hail to the vic-tors val-iant! Hail to the con-q'ring he-roes! Hail Hail _____ to

Mich-i-gan, the lead-ers and best. _____ Cham-pions of the West! _____ We cheer then a-

gain, For Mich-i-gan! We cheer with might and

main. We cheer, cheer, cheer, With might and main we cheer!

CODA Cham-pions of the West. _____

WALKABOUT
(From the Motion Picture "Walkabout")

Lyric by DON BLACK
Music by JOHN BARRY

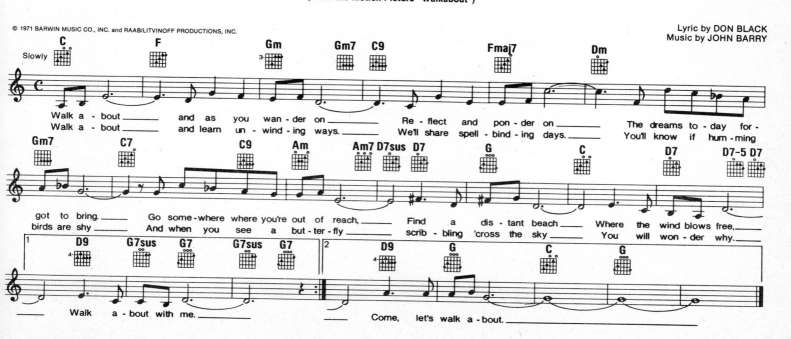

Walk a-bout _____ and as you wan-der on _____ Re-flect and pon-der on _____ The dreams to-day for-
Walk a-bout _____ and learn un-wind-ing ways. _____ We'll share spell-bind-ing days. _____ You'll know if hum-ming

got to bring. Go some-where where you're out of reach, _____ Find a dis-tant beach _____ Where the wind blows free, _____
birds are shy _____ And when you see a but-ter-fly _____ scrib-ling 'cross the sky _____ You will won-der why.

Walk a-bout with me. _____ Come, let's walk a-bout. _____

VICTORY RAG

By JAMES SCOTT

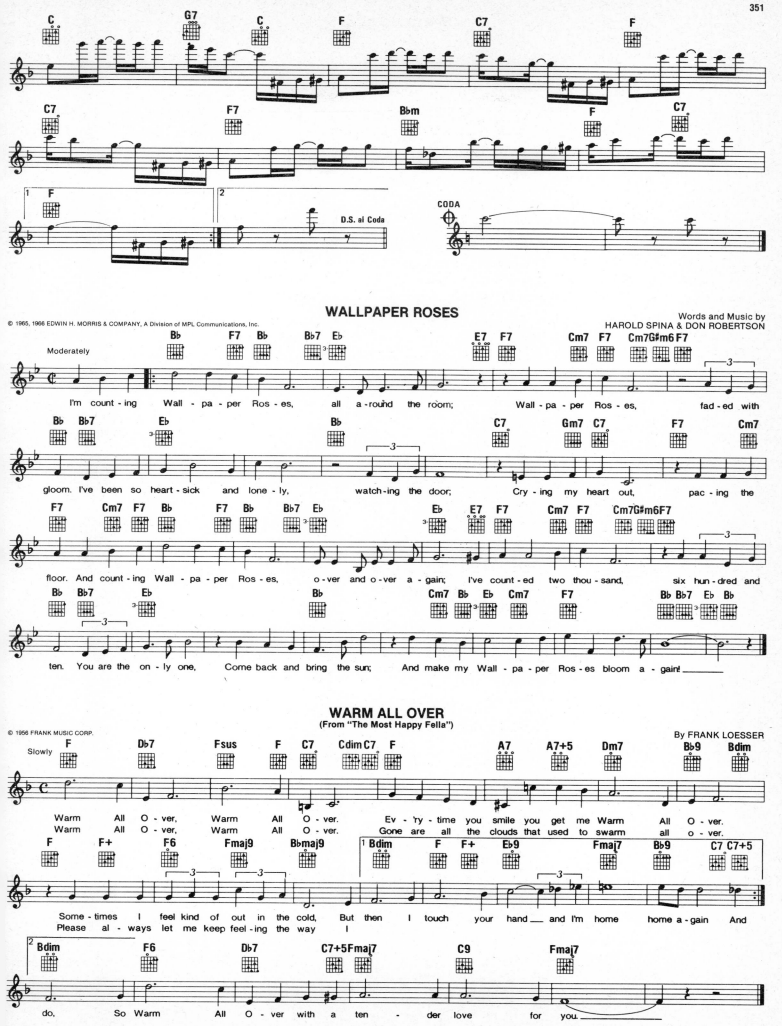

WALLPAPER ROSES

Words and Music by
HAROLD SPINA & DON ROBERTSON

WARM ALL OVER
(From "The Most Happy Fella")

By FRANK LOESSER

VAYA CON DIOS
(May God Be With You)

Words and Music by LARRY RUSSELL,
INEZ JAMES & BUDDY PEPPER

WHAT I DID FOR LOVE
(From "A Chorus Line")

Music by MARVIN HAMLISCH
Lyric by EDWARD KLEBAN

WHATEVER LOLA WANTS (Lola Gets)
(From "Damn Yankees")

Words and Music by
RICHARD ADLER & JERRY ROSS

WAS THAT THE HUMAN THING TO DO?

Words by JOE YOUNG
Music by SAMMY FAIN

WATERFALLS

Words and Music by
McCARTNEY

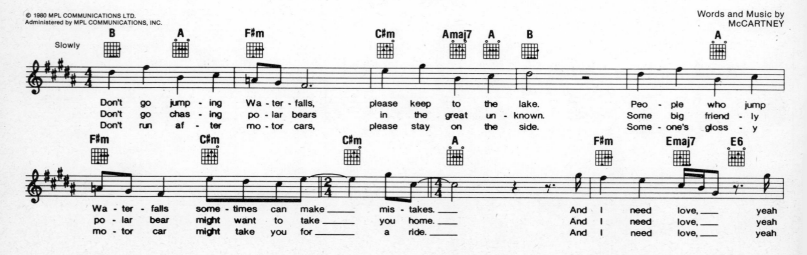

WAVE THE FLAG

By GORDON ERICKSON

WATERLOO

Words and Music by
JOHN LOUDERMILK & MARIJOHN WILKIN

Verse Brightly

Now old Ad - am _____ was the first in his - to - ry, With an ap - ple _____ he was
(Lit - tle) Gen - 'ral _____ Na - po - le - on of France Tried to con - quer _____ the

tempt - ed and de - ceived; Just for spite, the dev - il made him take a bite And that's where old Ad - am
world but lost his chance; Met de - feat, known as Bon - a - part's re - treat, And that's where Na - po - leon

met his Wa - ter - loo. _____ Wa - ter - loo, _____ Wa - ter - loo, _____ Where will
met his Wa - ter - loo.

you meet your Wa - ter - loo? _____ Ev - 'ry pup - py had its day, ev - 'ry - bod - y has to

pay, Ev - 'ry - bod - y has to meet his Wa - ter - loo. _____ Lit - tle Loo. _____

WE THREE
(My Echo, My Shadow And Me)

Lyric and Music by
DICK ROBERTSON, NELSON COGANE
& SAMMY MYSELS

Moderately

We Three _ we're all a - lone, Liv - ing in a mem - o - ry, My Ech - o, _ My Shad - ow _ And Me _____ We
Three, _ we're not a crowd, We're not e - ven com - pa - ny, My Ech - o, _ My

Shad - ow _ And Me. _ What good is the moon - light, The sil - ver - y moon - light that shines a - bove? _ I

walk with my shad - ow, I talk with my ech - o, But where is the one I love? We Three, _ we'll wait for you,

Ev - en 'till e - ter - ni - ty, My Ech - o, _ My Shad - ow _ And Me. _____

WE NEED A LITTLE CHRISTMAS
(From the Musical Production "Mame")

Music and Lyric by
JERRY HERMAN

WELL ALL RIGHT

Words and Music by
NORMAN PETTY, BUDDY HOLLY, JERRY ALLISON
& JOE MAULDIN

WEDDING BELLS

By CLAUDE BOONE

Wed - ding Bells are ring - ing in the cha - pel _____ That should be ring - ing now for you and me. _____ L
Wed - ding Bells are ring - ing in the cha - pel, _____ I hear the child - ren laugh - ing now with glee. _____ At
Wed - ding Bells are ring - ing in the cha - pel. _____ Ev - er since the day you set me free _____ I

Down the aisle with some - one else you're walk - ing _____ So, Wed - ding Bells will nev - er ring for me. _____
home a - lone I hang my head in sor - row. _____ Those Wed - ding Bells will nev - er ring for me. _____
knew some day that you would wed an - oth - er, _____ But Wed - ding Bells will nev - er ring for me. _____

WE GO TOGETHER
(From the Musical Production "Grease")

Lyric and Music by
WARREN CASEY & JIM JACOBS

We Go To - geth - er, like ra - ma la - ma la - ma ka ding - a da ding - dong, Re - mem - bered for - ev - er as
We're one of a kind like dip da dip _ da dip doo wop - a doo-bee doo, our _ names are signed

shoo - bop - sha - wad - da wad - da yip - pi - ty boom _ de - boom
boog-e-dy boog-e-dy booge-dy booge-dy shoo - by doo wop _ she bop

chang chang ah chang-it-ty chang - shoo bop, that's the way it should be, _ wha
chang chang ah chang-it-ty chang - shoo bop, we'll al - ways bee - ee like

oooh, yeah! one. Wa - wa - wa - waaah. _ When we go out at night,

and stars are shin - ing bright up in the skies a - bove. _____ Or at the

high school dance, where you can find ro - mance, may - be it might be love. _____

We're for each oth - er like-a wop ba-ba lu-mop and wop bam boom. _ Just like my broth - er is sha-na-na na-na-na,

WE MAKE A BEAUTIFUL PAIR
(From the Musical Production "Shenandoah")

Lyric by PETER UDELL
Music by GARY GELD

WEARY BLUES

Lyric by MORT GREENE & GEORGE CATES
Music by ARTIE MATTHEWS

THE WELLS FARGO WAGON
(From the Musical Production "The Music Man")

By MEREDITH WILLSON

once I got some grape-fruit from Tam-pa.____ Mont-gom-'ry Ward sent me a bath-tub and a cross-cut saw. O-ho, the
hope I get my rais-ins from Fres-no.____ The D. A. R. have sent a can-non for the court-house square. O-ho, the

Wells Far-go Wag-on is a - com-in' now. Is it a pre-paid sur-prise or C. O. D.? It could be
Wells Far-go Wag-on is a - com-in' now, I don't know how I can ev-er wait to see. It could be

cur-tains, or dish-es, or a dou-ble boil-er, Or it could be __ some-thin' spe-cial just for me.____ O-ho the
some-thin' from some-one who is no re-la-tion, but it could be __ some-thin' spe-cial just for me.____

WHAT DO YOU DO IN THE INFANTRY

By FRANK LOESSER

What Do You Do In The In-fant-ry? You march, you march, you march. What do you do when your pack has got your
What Do You Do In The In-fant-ry? You hike, you hike, you hike. What do you get in the In-fant-ry? A

back as stiff as starch?____ There's man-y a fall in the Cav-al-ry, but nev-er a fall-en arch ____ And
left and right ob-lique.____ The son-of-a-gun in the Sig-nal Corps is trav-el-ing on a bike ____ And

What Do You Do In The In-fant-ry? You march, you march, you march!
What Do You Do In The In-fant-ry? You hike, you hike, you hike!____ The hard way,____ the hard

way ____ Sweat 'til you get there the hard way! What Do You Do In The In-fant-ry? You win, you win, you

win What do you do for the Vic-tor-y? You move in-to Ber-lin.____ The rest of the Ar-my are

rid-ing, rid-ing thru a tri-umph-al arch ____ And What Do You Do In The In-fant-ry? You march! (Two,

three, four,) March! (Two, three, four,) March!____

WEDDING BELLS
(Are Breaking Up That Old Gang Of Mine)

Words by IRVING KAHAL
& WILLIE RASKIN
Music by SAMMY FAIN

Not a soul down on the cor - ner, That's a pret - ty cer - tain sign, That Wed - ding Bells are break - ing up __ that
boys are sing - ing love songs, They for - got "Sweet A - de - line" Those Wed - ding Bells are break - ing up __ that

old gang of mine. __ All the old gang of mine. There goes Jack, __ There goes Jim, __ Down to lov - er's lane, __

Now and then __ we meet a - gain, __ But they don't seem the same, __ Gee I get a lone - some feel - ing, When I

hear the church bells chime, __ Those Wed - ding Bells __ are break - ing up __ that old gang of mine.

WHAT ARE WE DOIN' IN LOVE

Words and Music by
RANDY GOODRUM

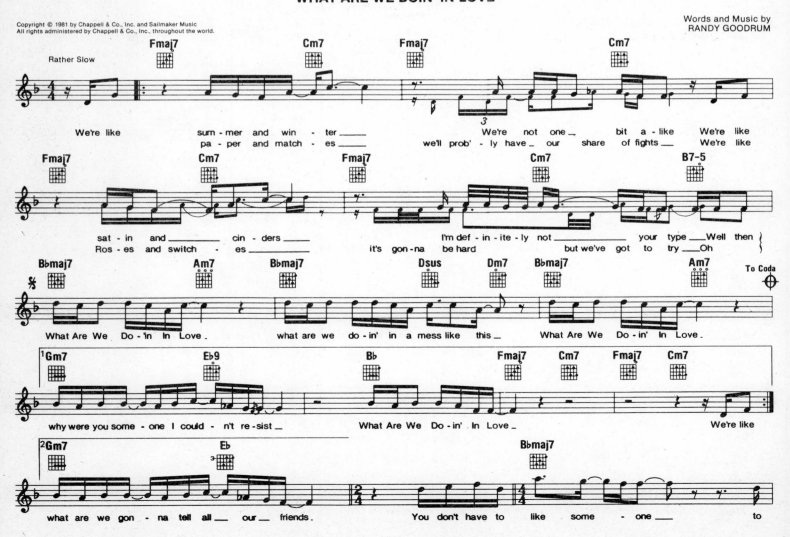

We're like sum - mer and win - ter ___ We're not one __ bit a - like We're like
pa - per and match - es ___ we'll prob' - ly have __ our share of fights ___ We're like

sat - in and ___ cin - ders ___ I'm def - in - ite - ly not ___ your type ___ Well then
Ros - es and switch - es ___ it's gon - na be hard but we've got to try ___ Oh

What Are We Do - in' In Love ___ what are we do - in' in a mess like this __ What Are We Do - in' In Love ___

why were you some - one I could - n't re - sist ___ What Are We Do - in' In Love ___ We're like

what are we gon - na tell all __ our friends. You don't have to like some - one ___ to

love some - one ___ That rule was made to be bro - ken ___ But if we have to

say good - bye to a life we've got - ten used to What Are We Do - in' In Love ___ Then ___ We're like

sun - up and sun - down ___ peo-ple say we're nev - er gon - na last We're like up - town and down - town ___

you like it slow and I like it fast So what are we gon - na tell all ___ our friends. What Are We Do - in' In Love.

what are we do - in' in a mess like this ___ What Are We Do - in' In Love ___

what are we gon - na tell all ___ our friends. That's what we're do - in' in lo - ve.

WENDY
(From "Peter Pan")

Lyric by BETTY COMDEN
& ADOLPH GREEN
Music by JULE STYNE

Moderately

Let's be qui - et as a mouse and build a love - ly lit - tle house for Wen - dy, ___ all for Wen - dy, ___ she's come to
Home sweet home up - on the wall, a wel - come mat down in the hall for Wen - dy, ___ so that Wen - dy ___

stay. ___ ___ won't go a - way. ___ Oh, the pleas - ure she'll bring to us, make us pock - ets

and sing to us, tell us sto - ries we've been long - ing to hear, o - ver and o - ver.

She'll be wait - ing at the door, we won't be lone - ly an - y - more, since Wen - dy, ___ love - ly Wen - dy's here to stay. ___

WHAT ARE YOU DOING NEW YEAR'S EVE

By FRANK LOESSER

WHEN MABEL COMES IN THE ROOM
(From "Mack and Mabel")

Music and Lyric by
JERRY HERMAN

WHEN JOANNA LOVED ME

WHEN THE SUN COMES OUT

Lyric by TED KOEHLER
Music by HAROLD ARLEN

WHEN THE IRISH BACKS GO MARCHING BY

Lyric by REV. EUGENE BURKE, C.S.C. '06
Music by JOSEPH J. CASASANTA

WHEN THE LIGHTS GO ON AGAIN
(All Over The World)

Words and Music by
EDDIE SEILER, SOL MARCUS
& BENNIE BENJAMIN

(How I'll Miss You)
WHEN THE SUMMER IS GONE

By HAL KEMP

WHERE DID ROBINSON CRUSOE GO WITH FRIDAY ON SATURDAY NIGHT?

Words by SAM M. LEWIS
& JOE YOUNG
Music by GEO. W. MEYER

WHEN VANDY STARTS TO FIGHT!
(The Dynamite Song)

Words and Music by
FRANCIS CRAIG

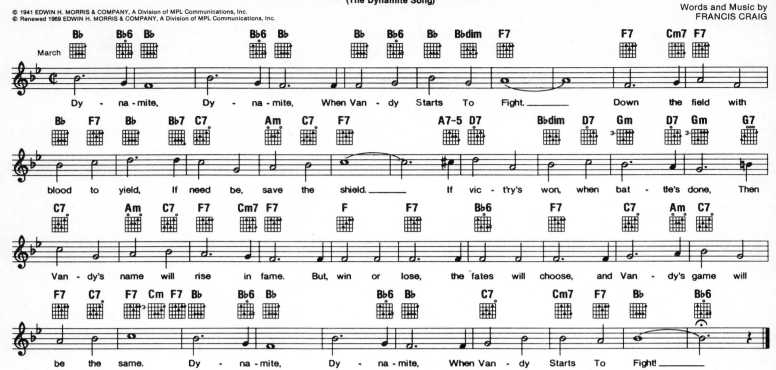

WITCHCRAFT

Lyric by CAROLYN LEIGH
Music by CY COLEMAN

WINTER ROSE / LOVE AWAKE

Words and Music by
McCARTNEY

WHY DID I CHOOSE YOU?
(From The Broadway Musical "The Yearling")

Lyric by HERBERT MARTIN
Music by MICHAEL LEONARD

WHY DON'T YOU DO RIGHT
(Get Me Some Money, Too!)

Words and Music by
JOE McCOY

would-n't be __ wand - 'ring now from do' to do', __ Why Don't You Do Right, _____ Like some oth - er men do?

Get out of here and get me some mon - ey too. _____ Why Don't You Do Right _____

_____ Like some oth - er men do? _____ Like some oth - er men do? _____

WHEN YOUR HAIR HAS TURNED TO SILVER
(I Will Love You Just The Same)

Lyric by CHARLIE TOBIAS
Music by PETER DeROSE

When Your Hair Has Turned To Sil - ver, _____ I will love you just the same; _____ I will on - ly call you

sweet - heart, _____ That will al - ways be your name. _____ Through a gar - den filled with ros - es _____ Down the sun - set

trail we'll stray: _____ When Your Hair Has Turned To Sil - ver _____ I will love you as to - day. _____

WHO ARE YOU?
(From the Motion Picture "The Great Waltz")

(Based on a Theme from "Die Fledermaus" by
JOHANN STRAUSS, JR.
Lyrics and Musical Adaptation by
ROBERT CRAIG WRIGHT & GEORGE FORREST

Who are you, Who are you, Stran - ger with search - ing eyes? Who are you? Whom are you Hop - ing to hyp - no - tize?

Is it I, Lone - ly I, By some en - chant - ed chance? Should it be, If it's so, Then it's love, And we'll go

Some - where a - part and a - far, Where I will live life through, Learn - ing who you are. _____ are.

A WOMAN ALONE WITH THE BLUES

© 1955, 1961 EDWIN H. MORRIS & COMPANY, A Division of MPL Communications, Inc.

Words and Music by
WILLARD ROBISON

WONDERFUL CHRISTMASTIME

© 1979 MPL COMMUNICATIONS LTD.
Administered by MPL COMMUNICATIONS, INC. by arrangement with WELBECK MUSIC CORP.

Words and Music by
McCARTNEY

WONDERFUL COPENHAGEN
(From "Hans Christian Andersen")

By FRANK LOESSER

WITH A LITTLE LUCK

Words and Music by
McCARTNEY

WITH THE WIND AND THE RAIN IN YOUR HAIR

Words and Music by
JACK LAWRENCE & CLARA EDWARDS

WOLVERINE BLUES

Words and Music by
JOHN SPIKES, BENJAMIN SPIKES
& FERD MORTON

YELLOW BIRD

Lyric by MARILYN KEITH
& ALAN BERGMAN
Music by NORMAN LUBOFF

THE WORST THAT COULD HAPPEN

Words and Music by
JIM WEBB

WILL WE EVER KNOW EACH OTHER
(From the Broadway Musical "The First")

Lyric by MARTIN CHARNIN
Music by BOB BRUSH

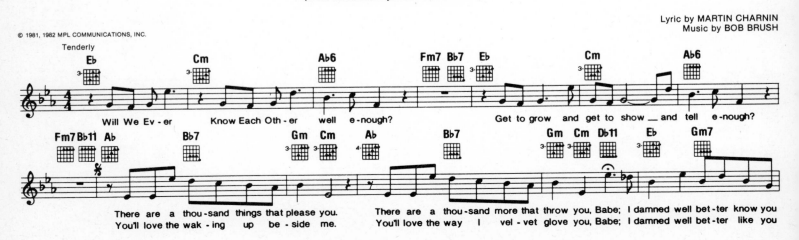

With humor

bet - ter than I know you.
bet - ter than I "love" you.

You know me, no drink - ing, no smok - ing, and I'm gor - geous,

You know me, your he - ro, we'd make ter - ri - fic ba - bies.

We may nev - er know each oth - er well e - nough;

There may nev - er be the time to tell e - nough.

But we have got to start out some - where.

(No need to start the need - ing of you, Babe. ___

How could I love you an - y bet - ter than I love you?

YOU GAVE ME THE ANSWER

Words and Music by
McCARTNEY

Moderately Bright

You Gave Me The An - swer_ to love_ e - ter - nal - ly; ___ I love you and you, you seem_ to like

me. Wher - ev - er we wan - der,_ the lo - cal folk a - gree;_ I love_ you and _

you, you seem_ to like me. Head - ing back_ to old_ fa - mil - iar plac - es; _____ Plac - es where the

cob - webs blown a - way;_ I _ can for get the airs_ and grac - es. _____ Mm. ___ You'll nev - er be

crowned by _ the ar - is - toc - ra - cy _____ To their de - light,_ you'd mere - ly in vite them in ____ for a cup of tea, _

_____ and I love you, and you, you seem_ to like, you seem_ to like, you seem_ to like me. _____

THE WOMAN IN ME

Words and Music by
SUSAN MARIE THOMAS

Seems to me no mat-ter what I do I pick the wrong time to do it In a min-ute I will be al-right if you will
Can I help it if it feels good to have your arms wrapped a-round me. When you touch me I'm a lit-tle girl and there's so

let me think it through I could comb my hair and walk right out of here so fast Let the si-lence tell you that I've
much that I still need Give me room to touch my own heart I'm not so weak I could fly a-way and leave you

grown up at last You'll nev-er break The Wo-man In Me though you might break a smile You'll nev-er hurt The Wo-man In Me but
A kiss on the cheek.

you might hurt the child You'll nev-er break The Wo-man In Me though

you might break a smile You'll nev-er hurt The Wo-man In Me but you might hurt the child

YOUNG AND WARM AND WONDERFUL

Lyric by HY ZARET
Music by LOU SINGER

Young And Warm And Won-der-ful You are all I dreamed you'd be.

Dreams that seemed im-pro-ba-ble All at once have come true, now I see, Ev-'ry

search-ing heart finds its hap-pi-ness; Love is on-ly a mat-ter of time.

Young And Warm And Won-der-ful, At last you're here, my love, And love is mine.

WHY DO THEY ALL TAKE THE NIGHT BOAT TO ALBANY?

© 1918 MILLS MUSIC, INC.
© Renewed 1946 MPL COMMUNICATIONS, INC. and WAROCK CORP.

Words by SAM M. LEWIS
& JOE YOUNG
Music by JEAN SCHWARTZ

A WOMAN IN LOVE
(From "Guys And Dolls")

© 1955 FRANK MUSIC CORP.

By FRANK LOESSER

YA GOT TROUBLE
(From "The Music Man")

By MEREDITH WILLSON

Bright 2

Ab7

Well ya got trou-ble, my friend___ right here I say trou-ble right here in Riv-er Cit-y. Why sure, I'm a

bil-liard play-er, cer-tain-ly might-y proud, I say I'm al-ways might-y proud to say it.

Bbm7 **Eb7** **Bbm7** **F#m6** **Eb7**

I con-sid-er that the hours I spend with a cue in my hand are gold-en. Help you cul-ti-vate

Bbm7 **Eb7** **Bbm7** **Gbdim** **Gdim** **Ab6** Tacet

horse sense and a cool head and a keen eye. 'Jev-er take-'n try to give an

Ab7 **E7** **Eb7** **Ab**

i-ron clad leave to your-self from a three-rail bill-iard___ shot? But just as I say, it takes judg-ment,

brains and ma-tur-i-ty to score in a balk-line game I say that an-y boob_____ kin take 'n' shove a

Db6 ⌐3⌐ **Ddim** **Ab**

ball in a pock-et, And I call that sloth!___ The first big step on the road to the depths of de-gra-

Gb **F7+5** **F7** **Bb7** **Eb7**

da___ I say, first it's a lit-tle ah, me-dic-i-nal wine from a tea-spoon; Then___ beer from a bot-tle. And the

Ab

next thing you know, your son is play-in' fer mon-ey in a pinch-back suit, and list'-nin' to some big out-

Adim **Bbm7** **Adim** **Bbm7** **Eb7** **Bbm7**

_____a-town jas-per hear-in' him tell a-bout horse-race gamb-lin'. Not a whole-some trot-tin' race, no! But a

Gbm6 **Eb7** **Bbdim** **Fb7** **Ab**

race where they se' down right on a horse! Like to see some stuck-up jock-ey boy set-tin' on Dan

YES, MY DARLING DAUGHTER

Words and Music by
JACK LAWRENCE

YOU CALL IT MADNESS
(But I Call It Love)

By CON CONRAD, GLADYS DU BOIS,
RUSS COLUMBO & PAUL GREGORY

YOU'RE THE REASON GOD MADE OKLAHOMA

Words and Music by
SANDY PINKARD & LARRY COLLINS

There's a full ___ moon o - ver Tul - sa I hope that it's shin - nin' on you ___ The nights are get - tin' cold - er in

Cher - o - kee coun - try there's a Blue Nor - ther pas - sin' through ___ I re - mem - ber green eyes, and a ranch - er's daugh - ter but re -

mem - ber is all that I do. ___ Los - in' you left ___ a pret - ty good cow - boy with noth - in' to hold ___ on

to. Sun - down came, and I drove ___ to town ___ and drank a drink ___ or two. ___

You're The Rea - son God Made ___ Ok - la - ho - ma. ___ You're The Rea - son God Made ___ Ok - la - ho - ma ___ And

I'm sure mis - sin' you ___ And I'm sure mis - sin' you. I'm sure mis - sin'

you. ___ I

CODA

I'm sure mis - sin' you ___ And I'm sure mis - sin' you.

2. Here the city lights outshine the moon
I was just now thinking of you
Sometimes when the wind blows you can see the mountains
And all the way to Malibu
Everyone's a star here in L.A. County
You ought to see the things that they do.
All the cowboys down on the Sunset Strip
Wish they could be like you.
The Santa Monica Freeway
Sometimes makes a country girl blue

(BRIDGE)

3. I worked ten hours on a John Deere tractor,
Just thinkin of you all day. . .
I've got a calico cat and a two
room flat, on a
street in West L.A.

YOU FASCINATE ME SO

Lyric by CAROLYN LEIGH
Music by CY COLEMAN

Moderately

I have a feel - ing that be - neath the lit - tle ha - lo on your no - ble head ___
I feel like Christ - o - pher Co - lum - bus when I'm near e - nough to con - tem - plate ___

There lies a thought or two the dev - il might be in - t'rest - ed to know ___
The sweet ge - og - ra - phy de - scend - ing from your eye - brow to your toe ___

You're like the fin - ish of a
The pos - si - bil - i - ties are

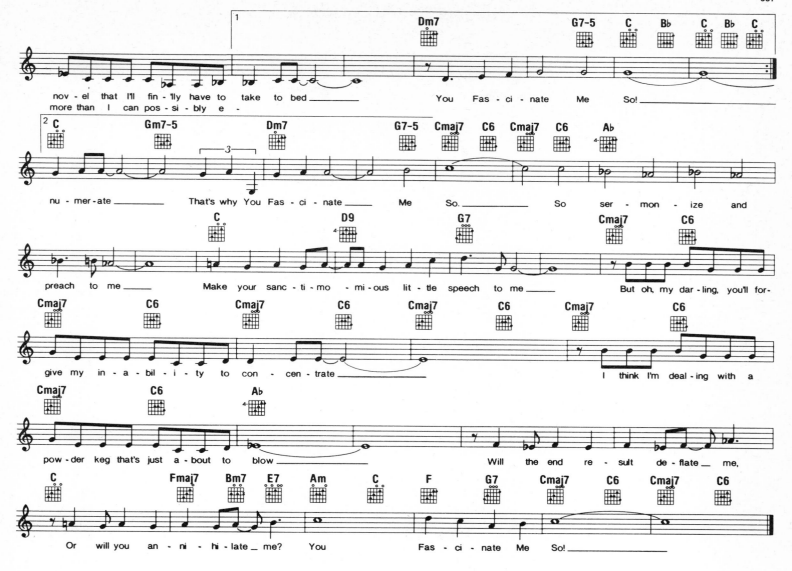

YOU'RE MY EVERYTHING

Words by MORT DIXON
& JOE YOUNG
Music by HARRY WARREN

You Call Everybody Darling

By SAM MARTIN, BEN TRACE
& CLEM WATTS

YOU MADE ME LOVE YOU

Words by JOE McCARTHY
Music by JAMES V. MONACO

YOU'RE NO GOOD

Words and Music by
CLINT BALLARD, JR.

YOU WANTED SOMEONE TO PLAY WITH
(I Wanted Someone To Love)

Lyric by FRANK CAPANO
& MARGIE MORRIS
Music by GEORGE B. McCONNELL
& NAT OSBORNE

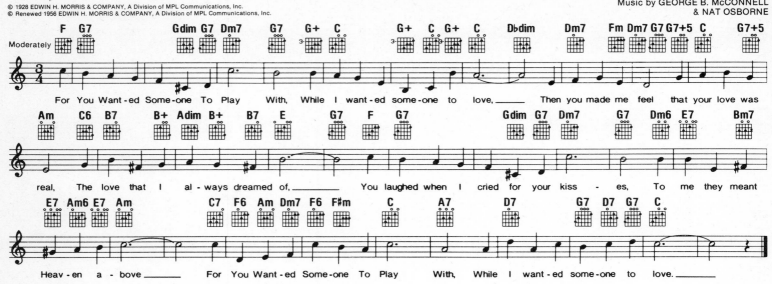

For You Want-ed Some-one To Play With, While I want-ed some-one to love,_____ Then you made me feel that your love was

real, The love that I al-ways dreamed of,_____ You laughed when I cried for your kiss-es, To me they meant

Heav-en a-bove_____ For You Want-ed Some-one To Play With, While I want-ed some-one to love._____

YOUR CHEATIN' HEART

Words and Music by
HANK WILLIAMS

Your Cheat-in'___ Heart_____ will make you weep You'll cry and_ cry_____ and try to
Your Cheat-in'___ Heart_____ will pine some-day_____ And crave the_ love_____ you threw a-

sleep_____ But sleep won't come_____ the whole night through_____ Your Cheat-in'___ Heart
way_____ The time will_ come_____ when you'll be blue_____ Your Cheat-in'___ Heart

___ will tell on you_____ When tears come down_____ like fall-in' rain_____ You'll toss a-
___ will tell on you_____ When tears come down_____ like fall-in' rain_____ You'll toss a-

round_____ and call my name_____ You'll walk the_ floor_____ the way I do_____
round_____ and call my name_____ You'll walk the_ floor_____ the way I do_____

___ Your Cheat-in'___ Heart_____ will tell on you. Your Cheat-in'
___ Your Cheat-in'___ Heart_____ will tell on you._____

YOU'VE COME HOME
(From the Musical Production "Wildcat")

Lyric by CAROLYN LEIGH
Music by CY COLEMAN

YOUNG AT HEART

Words by CAROLYN LEIGH
Music by JOHNNY RICHARDS

YOU'RE NEVER FULLY DRESSED WITHOUT A SMILE

(From the Musical Production "Annie")

Lyric by MARTIN CHARNIN
Music by CHARLES STROUSE

YOUR FEET'S TOO BIG

Words and Music by
ADA BENSON & FRED FISHER

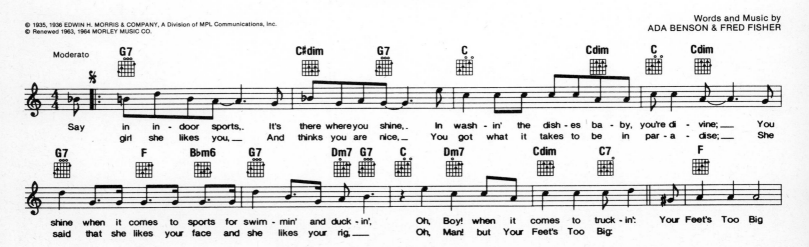

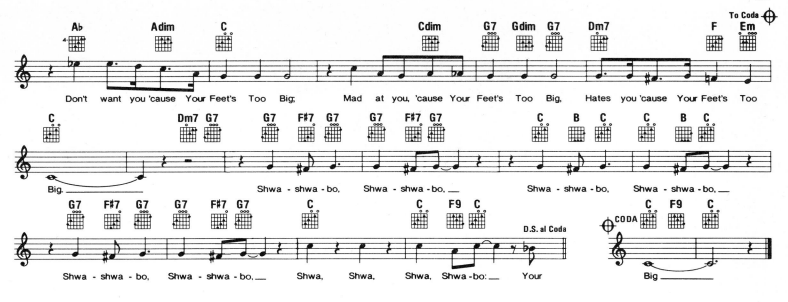

YOU WIN AGAIN

Words and Music by
HANK WILLIAMS

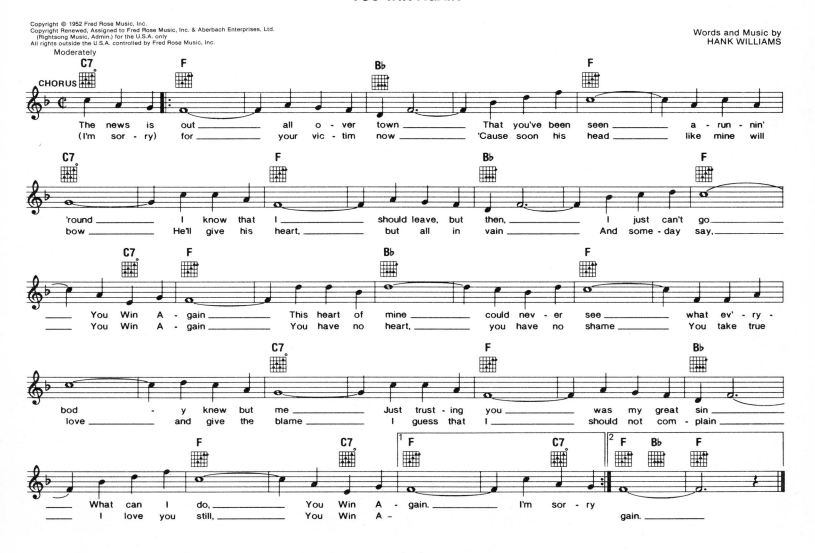

CHORD INVERSION CHART

This chart illustrates the best inversions for keeping the left hand within a "one octave" position.

	D♭(C♯)	A♭	E♭	B♭	F	C
MAJOR						
MINOR						
7th						
DIM.						
AUG.						
MIN. 7th						
6th						
9th						
MIN. 6th						
MAJOR 7th						

Piano Chord Chart

	G	D	A	E	B	F#(Gb)
MAJOR	G 5 3 1	D 5 3 1	A 5 3 1	E 5 3 1	B 5 2 1	F#(Gb) 5 3 1
MINOR	Gm 5 3 1	Dm 5 2 1 / 5 3 1	Am 5 3 1	Em 5 3 1	Bm 5 2 1	F#m(Gbm) 5 3 1
7th	G7 5 3 2 1 / 5 4 2 1	D7 5 3 2 1 / 5 3 2 1	A7 5 4 2 1	E7 5 3 2 1	B7 5 3 2 1	F#7(Gb7) 5 3 2 1
DIM.	Gdim 5 3 2 1	Ddim 5 3 2 1	Adim 5 3 2 1	Edim 5 3 2 1	Bdim 5 3 2 1	F#(Gb)dim 5 3 2 1
AUG.	G+ 5 3 1	D+ 5 3 1	A+ 5 3 1 / 5 3 1	E+ 5 2 1	B+ 5 3 1	F#+(Gb+) 5 3 1
MIN.7th	Gm7 5 3 2 1	Dm7 5 3 2 1 / 5 3 21	Am7 5 4 2 1	Em7 5 3 2 1	Bm7 5 3 2 1	F#(Gb)m7 5 4 2 1
6th	G6 5 3 2 1	D6 5 3 2 1	A6 5 4 2 1	E6 5 3 2 1	B6 5 4 2 1	F#6(Gb6) 5 3 2 1
9th	G9 5 3 2 1 / 5 4 2 1	D9 5 3 2 1	A9 5 3 2 1	E9 5 4 2 1	B9 5 4 2 1	F#9(Gb9) 5 4 2 1
MIN.6th	Gm6 5 3 2 1	Dm6 5 4 2 1 / 5 3 2 1	Am6 5 3 2 1	Em6 5 3 2 1	Bm6 5 4 2 1	F#(Gb)m6 5 4 2 1
MAJOR 7th	Gmaj7 5 3 2 1	Dmaj7 5 3 1	Amaj7 5 3 1	Emaj7 5 3 1	Bmaj7 5 3 1	F#(Gb)maj7 5 3 2 1

NOTES